REWARD

Collect Millions for Reporting Tax Evasion

Joel D. Hesch, Esq.

LU
Books

Published and printed in the United States of America

First edition
ISBN: 978-0-9819357-2-0

Business/Money/Finance

LCCN: 2008909933

LU Books
A Division of Liberty University Press
1971 University Blvd., Lynchburg, VA 24502
434-592-2000
www.LibertyUniversityPress.com

Disclaimers. The views expressed by the author are his own personal opinions and beliefs and do not represent the views of the Department of Justice (DOJ), the Internal Revenue Service (IRS), or Liberty University School of Law, where the author is a professor.

Although portions of this book are based in part upon true cases, the names and facts have been altered in order to best illustrate points to aid in your understanding of the government reward programs. Therefore, even if you think you recognize a case used as an illustration, it is not intended to represent a particular case.

This book should not be construed as legal advice. Each case is unique and must be evaluated on its own merits. Past amounts of recoveries do not guarantee future rewards. You should consult an attorney experienced with government reward programs before deciding whether to file for a reward.

Publisher's Cataloging-in-Publication
(Provided by Quality Books, Inc.)

Hesch, Joel D.
    Reward : collecting millions for reporting tax
evasion : your complete guide to the IRS whistleblower
reward program / Joel Hesch.
    p. cm.
    Includes bibliographical references and index.
    LCCN 2008909933
    ISBN-13: 978-0-9772602-3-2
    ISBN-10: 0-9819357-2-9

    1. Whistle blowing. 2. Fraud—United States.
3. United States--Claims. 4. Public contracts—United
States. 5. Popular actions—United States. I. Title.

JF1525.W45H47 2008   353.4'6
                        QBI08-600314

Acknowledgement

I am grateful to my lovely wife, Theresa, for her faithfulness and support.

You will want to thank her too, as she encouraged me to reduce the length of the main text by about 30 pages in order to get to the meat sooner and also to keep a conversational tone—free from legalese. So you wouldn't miss out on anything, however, I included the omitted material in appendices, loading them with examples and resources so you can get a complete picture of the program and know how to submit a winning application for a reward.

Contents

Preface

Patriotism is easy to understand in America. It means looking out for yourself by looking out for your country.

— CALVIN COOLIDGE (1872–1933)

The only thing worse than paying your own taxes is paying someone else's taxes. Right now, you are paying $1,000 a year more in taxes that you should because corporations and individuals are committing tax evasion.

The difference between the amount of federal taxes legally owed and the amount actually collected by the Internal Revenue Service (IRS) is referred to as "the tax gap." According to the Government Accounting Office (GAO), corporations and individuals collectively under-report their taxes by $340 billion every year. That means the tax gap is 15%.

Tax evasion is out of control. Over the years, the old methods used by the IRS to curtail the growing problem with tax evasion stopped working. The threat of an IRS audit lost its sting. As a result, the IRS gradually cut back on the number of audits in some areas, even while tax evasion continued to grow.

In response, Congress passed a law that required the IRS to increase rewards to citizens who team up with the IRS by reporting tax evasion. It mandated that the IRS start paying million-dollar rewards to citizens who turn in income tax cheaters.

The new law requires that the IRS form a dedicated Whistleblower Reward Office to pay rewards of 15% to 30% of whatever it recovers—no matter how large the amount is—based on the information it receives from citizen like you. You win a lucrative reward and the IRS wins too, because it not only cracks down on tax cheats, but it gets to keep the rest of the money. With this new law, Congress ensures that the terms are very generous to the citizens who report tax evasion, since any money recovered is money the IRS would not have collected otherwise. The program is not limited to corporate tax cheaters. It equally applies when individuals fail to pay the full amount of taxes owed.

The Reward Program goes like this. Suppose the company you work for cheats on its taxes by $10 million. You report it, following the steps laid out in this book. The IRS investigates and collects the money. You get between $2 million and $3 million. What's not to love?

You don't need to prove fraud or intentional cheating on taxes in order to get a reward. The IRS, however, gets most excited about fraudulent tax returns (which, by the way, do not have a statute of limitation). But a reward is also available if the IRS recovers "unpaid taxes" within the time limit it has to conduct an audit, based upon your report.

This means that even if you know of a company or individual making unacceptable deductions based on advice from an accountant, you can make a report based on your reasonable skepticism of the legitimacy of the deduction. If the IRS finds that the deductions were not allowable and collects money, you share in the recovery.

The good news about this program is that the IRS is committed to maintaining its confidences. In most cases, your name will never be revealed, even if you receive a $100 million reward.

You can also have an attorney help you file the claim and negotiate the amount of your reward with the IRS. Should the IRS attempt to give you a reward that is too low, your attorney can challenge the amount in federal Tax Court.

Of course, if you are rewarded with $2 million or $3 million, you'll have to pay taxes on that money. But it's better than paying $1,000 extra every year to make up for other people's tax evasion—without doing anything about it. And it hurts a lot less to pay the IRS taxes on millions of dollars they've given you in the first place.

Introduction:
Obtaining an IRS Reward

You must pay the price if you wish to secure the blessing.
— ANDREW JACKSON (1767–1845)

You have a lot to be excited about. Congress has mandated that the IRS pay multi-million dollar rewards to anyone reporting tax evasion—rather than pouring more money into ineffective random audits that are incapable of detecting tax fraud.

Because you can receive 15% to 30% of the money recovered, the sky is the limit for what you can be paid by stepping forward.

Before rushing to file for a reward under the new IRS Reward Program, however, you must understand the requirements. Like most things bureaucratic, if you do not strictly follow the rules and meet the standards, you cannot receive a reward. There are also informal or unwritten rules which the IRS follows when deciding whether or how much of a reward to pay. In short, there is a lot more involved than simply calling a hotline or filling out a one-page form.

This chapter provides an outline introducing the risks, requirements, and rewards of reporting tax evasion so that you now can begin evaluating your case and submit a winning application. The rest of the book will be your detailed roadmap for identifying cases where significant rewards are possible, properly preparing the application, and calculating how much of a reward you may receive.

Understanding the New IRS Reward Program

The new IRS Reward Program was not developed in a vacuum. It has a history. In fact, the old IRS program, which was put into law 140 years ago, is still intact and applies in instances where a person fails to meet all of the requirements of the new program. You definitely want to avoid that, because the old program is very restrictive.

The new IRS Reward Program is *so new* that there are no court cases to give you insights into how the program works. That's why the next chapter will outline the related U.S. Department of Justice (DOJ) Whistleblower Reward Program (or DOJ program for short). It has stood the test of nearly two decades and has numerous legal decisions that dictate responsibilities of the government in paying rewards and eligibility requirements of whistleblowers. Because the IRS program was modeled after it, the court cases for the DOJ program may be persuasive to the Tax Court in ruling on the IRS program.

Right after that, the second chapter will whet your appetite by exploring the largest tax evasion cases—the type where hundreds of millions of dollars in rewards are possible. Afterwards, the twin IRS programs will be introduced. This background is essential if you want to learn from the past in order to avoid making common mistakes in the future. You will want to pay attention, as the old program pays *less than half* what the new program pays.

This book also lists hundreds of areas ripe for rewards, including both domestic and offshore tax evasion. Having in mind actual examples of tax evasion will boost your appreciation for how the technical requirements work and alert you to the possibilities of tax evasion you may be able to report.

Would you like to get an idea of how much of a reward you may receive? An entire chapter is devoted to introducing you to the ranges of rewards and showing you how to estimate your potential reward.

To receive a reward, you must meet all of the technical requirements, as explained in Chapter Six. The key technical requirements are boiled down into the *"Four F Factors."*

In this book, you will also learn the secrets that will increase your chance of getting a reward. If all you do is meet the minimum technical requirements, it is doubtful you will receive a reward. Insiders know that there are also unspoken rules that greatly affect your chances of collecting a reward. This book will let you in on everything you need to know to be sure you meet these unspoken rules.

Throughout the book you will be given helpful hints, as well as checklists and practical advice on how to position yourself to increase the odds of claiming your reward. You will learn how to avoid common mistakes that may ruin your application and find out why the IRS rejects many cases. It will help you judge whether you would be wasting your time or whether you simply need to gather more information before filing for a reward.

The chapters build on each other, so it is best to read them in order. By the time you reach the checklists in Chapter Fifteen, you will be able to tell whether or not you have what you need to claim your own reward.

Ready to Begin?

This book will take you through a step-by-step process for creating an application—from start to finish. After that, it's up to you.

Are you ready to take the next step?

Chapter One
Other Government Reward Programs

All that is required for evil to prevail is for good men to do nothing.
— EDMUND BURKE (1729–1797)

Haven't you ever wished you could have just a small percentage of the money that big corporations save every year by cheating on their taxes? Now, you can.

After all these years of thinking of the IRS as a big bully, trying to nickel-and-dime you out of your last pennies every April 15, it may surprise you, but things have changed. Congress has now ordered the IRS to let you have a piece of the pie.

Instead of watching helplessly while rich people and corporations save billions of dollars with illegal tax schemes, you can receive 15% to 25% of that money yourself.

Hard to believe?

The new IRS Whistleblower Reward Program is for real. Million-dollar rewards are available to those who report the underpayment of taxes. You could be one of those who collect one of these generous rewards.

Of course, there is a catch: Once you find a tax cheat to report, you *must* prepare the application properly, or the IRS won't even consider your case.

That's where this book comes in. By the time you finish reading it, you will be armed with the information you need to prepare a viable submission for the IRS and get the help you need to increase your chances of success.

In this chapter, you will learn why the IRS is offering rewards, so you can understand how the program works, and in particular, why it makes sense for the IRS to pay such huge rewards. Knowing why the government has actually paid sizeable whistleblower rewards will peel away some of your distrust and even spark a glow of anticipation as the rest of this book unfolds and shows you exactly how to submit a winning application.

Legal Groundwork and Evidence of Paid Claims

Your interest in this program puts you on the cutting edge. The revamped IRS Reward Program described in this book is *so new* that there are no legal cases addressing any aspect of it. Programs like these always start with formal guidelines to follow, but as people start to use the program, the rules change and evolve. Lawsuits are filed, questioning various aspects of the wording. New terms are introduced. Old terms are clarified. Until a history of legal cases has built up, it is hard to know which aspects of the guidelines will stand up in court and which ones won't.

That leaves a lot of room to wonder how the program will actually work. However, you are in luck. Because the IRS Reward Program was modeled directly on the Department of Justice (DOJ) Reward Program, a lot of the legal groundwork for both of these programs has already been laid. There have been hundreds of court cases deciding many of the "who, what, where, when and how" questions of the DOJ Reward Program. So knowing about the DOJ program will help answer some of the questions and fill in some of the gaps of the new IRS program. (That's also why some later chapters discuss the DOJ program when answering questions about the meaning of certain aspects of the IRS program. Believe me, the similarity of these two programs gives you a significant advantage. It allows you to get in early and benefit from the IRS program far ahead of the curve.)

You Want Proof that It Works

The DOJ Reward Program also provides proof that you can truly collect a reward for reporting tax evasion. If you have been following the IRS track record of paying out rewards, you have good cause to wonder whether the IRS will actually pay you millions of dollars.

The truth is, the IRS has had the authority to pay rewards for 140 years. However, it has rarely paid large rewards. Is there any reason to believe this new program will be any different? Is there really a new face to the IRS—one inviting you to share in the rewards of tracking down tax evasion?

The answer is an unequivocal yes. There has been an important change. The DOJ Reward Program has paid out so much money to citizens who have identified cheats that the Department of Justice has recovered billions of dollars as a result. This is exciting news for the citizens making 15% to 30% of recoveries, but it is also good news for the government. As a result, Congress has now mandated that the IRS adopt the same program that has been so successful at the DOJ for the past twenty years. To spur the new program, it even required the IRS to pay a higher percentage to whistleblowers than the DOJ program! Congressional oversight will ensure that the IRS Reward Program works as much like the successful DOJ Reward Program as possible. So there is every reason to believe that the rewards in the two programs will be largely identical.

The Related DOJ Whistleblower Reward Program

Did you know that the DOJ Reward Program has already paid $3 billion in rewards to average citizens for stepping forward and reporting fraud? The largest reward for a single case was like winning the lottery for the happy whistleblower who received more than $150 million. But tax fraud is on the rise, so that record is waiting to be broken. Much larger rewards are available under the IRS program, if you know what to look for.

The similarities between the DOJ Reward Program and the new IRS Reward Program begin with the timing of when both were created. The initial DOJ program was enacted by Abraham Lincoln in 1863. The initial IRS Reward Program was enacted just four years later, in 1867. For more than 100 years, both programs mainly collected dust. They each had numerous problems and neither were whistleblower friendly.

However, in 1986, in the face of rising fraud against the government, the DOJ revamped and re-launched its Whistleblower Reward Program by adding a feature you can appreciate: It began to offer huge rewards for reporting fraud. It also began a new era of actually inviting whistleblowers to team with it. Congress authorized the DOJ to create a highly successful Whistleblower Reward Program by paying whistleblowers between 15% and 25% of what the government collects based on their reports.

With these benefits added, the DOJ Reward Program was a huge and immediate success. Whistleblowers are now responsible for most recoveries for fraud against the government. The amount of fraud being reported keeps growing and the amount of rewards keeps climbing. It is a win-win for everyone.

Consider the following statistics about the DOJ program, as of the end of 2008:

- 80% of government fraud cases were brought by whistleblowers
- $8.5 million was the average amount of fraud against the government in a whistleblower case
- 1 out of 5 whistleblowers received a reward
- 4 rewards topped $100 million, and 16 exceeded $50 million
- $1.5 million was the average reward

Why does DOJ keep paying record rewards? The answer is simple mathematics.

By paying out nearly $3 billion in rewards, the government reclaimed over $20 billion from companies cheating Medicare, the military and many other programs. That is a net return of over $17 billion, just for offering rewards. And the numbers keep rising every year, with DOJ now recovering roughly $2 billion a year and paying $500 million annually in rewards.

The sky is the limit to the amount of rewards the government can pay. Remember, the reward is a percentage of the fraud, so there is no cap on rewards paid. Each year, the federal government spends more than $2.5 trillion dollars. Under many of its programs, such as Medicare, it is losing 10% to fraud—translating into as much as $250 billion each year. Because the government catches less than 1% of corporate crooks who defraud federal government agencies—such as the military, the post office, Medicare, and Homeland Security—it is well worth it to pay a portion of what the federal government collects to the citizens who report fraud.

Now that the strategy has proven to be so spectacularly successful for the DOJ, the IRS has been required to do the same. Congress mandated that the IRS adopt a reward program similar to DOJ's. It is banking on paying billions of dollars in rewards for turning in tax cheats to put a big dent into the $350 billion lost annually due to those evading taxes.

It is time for you to get involved with combating tax evasion.

Chapter Two

A Quick Peek at the Largest IRS Tax Evasion Cases

Honor lies in honest toil.

— GROVER CLEVELAND (1837–1908)

When the new IRS Rewards Program was recently created, its new director, Stephen A. Whitlock, was asked to give an example of his "dream" application from a citizen reporting tax evasion. Smiling brightly, he said he longed for the day when he would be able to hand a person a huge check with lots of zeros—as if he were awarding the grand prize in a sweepstakes. He said his dream was to hold constant press conferences to announce the huge rewards the IRS was paying citizens for their help.

Incredible! Did you ever think you'd hear that the IRS was actually looking forward to paying extremely big rewards—the kind that make the local lottery seem small? This really is something new.

Mr. Whitlock was asked, "How big do you mean? Is a reward of $1 billion possible?" He hinted that not only was it possible, but very likely that someone would receive a billion-dollar reward. A person just needed to submit a proper application.

In light of the $350 billion tax gap, the director is right. If even a fraction of that money was collected and 15% to 30% was paid to citizens, a billion-dollar reward would not be just a dream, it would be a reality.

Are you ready for a sneak peak of a few whopper cases where the IRS has collected astronomical amounts against those underpaying taxes? Mega-rewards were not paid to individuals in these situations because the new IRS Reward Program did not yet exist. But just think—if you had known about the tax evasion and reported it, you would have been eligible for rewards of $135 million, $650 million, and $1 billion, respectively. There would also be additional rewards of $1 billion for reporting the individuals who paid $4 billion to settle tax shelter abuse allegations.

Accounting Firm Tax Evasion

In the largest criminal tax case ever filed, a large accounting firm pled guilty in a scheme that cost the government $2.5 billion dollars in evaded taxes.[2] The DOJ alleged that the accounting firm helped devise, market and implement improper tax shelters. Thousands used these phony shelters to improperly claim $11 billion in expenses that were not tax deductible and thereby underpaid taxes.

The IRS labels these types of inappropriate tax shelters as "Son of Boss" Shelters (since they are based on the original "BOSS," which stands for "Bond and Option Sales Strategy" tax scheme, where false losses in bonds and stock options are claimed as tax deductions). Here is how it works. Suppose Brian is a corporate executive for a huge company. Part of his compensation is the option to buy 10,000 shares of stock each year for $100 per share. Five years later, the stock rises considerably, selling for $300 a share. Brian now seeks to buy or redeem 50,000 shares of stock at $100 each and cash it out. He is willing to pay $5 million to buy stocks currently selling for $15 million. He also wants to cash out now and take a profit of $10 million. However, Brian does not want to pay taxes on the $10 million. His accountant uses a BOSS type shelter to conduct a complex series of transactions which makes it appear that there is both income and a loss of $10 million, so Brian does not need to pay any taxes on the stock options he redeemed and sold.

You may wonder how this type of a transaction could even appear proper. In the Son of Boss initiative, the government contended that an attorney received $50,000 for each letter he wrote to clients stating that the purported tax losses generated by the

BOSS shelters were "more likely than not" to withstand IRS scrutiny. That gave the clients the cover they needed should a routine audit be performed. Most auditors accepted the legal opinion and were otherwise unable to figure out the scheme. In short, the IRS alleged that the clients simply bought letters from attorneys in order to argue with the IRS in any subsequent audit that they believed the transactions were legitimate.

It worked for a while. However, eventually the IRS got wise and began disallowing deductions from BOSS shelters.

The large accounting firm in this case ended up agreeing to pay $456 million in settlement. The individual taxpayers who participated in the tax schemes were also on the hook for alleged tax evasion. The IRS collected an additional $4 billion from those taxpayers who agreed to participate in a global settlement offered by the IRS.

Offshore "Shell" Company

In 2007, a pharmaceutical company paid the IRS $2.3 billion to resolve allegations that it engaged in tax evasion. The IRS alleged that a large U.S. pharmaceutical company underpaid federal income taxes by transferring ownership of patents for two of its popular drugs to a shell company it formed in Bermuda. The IRS contended that the entity in Bermuda had no real employees and no real existence, except on paper. The IRS alleged that the transfer of the valuable patent was a sham and the Bermuda company did not pay fair market value for the income-producing asset. Rather, the transfer was to avoid paying taxes.

How does a company cheat on taxes by shifting title or ownership of property overseas? The offshore company leases back to the U.S. company the right to sell the items in the U.S. It charges the American company approximately the same price in fees as it expects to receive from selling the items. Thus, the U.S. company reports virtually no income, because it deducts the lease prices from the sales prices. The offshore company, however, makes billions of dollars from the leases. It does not have to report this as income because foreign companies are not subject to the U.S. tax laws. In addition, the tax haven country charges little, if any, income tax on this type of transaction.

In the pharmaceutical example, the IRS contended that the Bermuda company was improperly charging its U.S. counterpart company huge royalties for purportedly being allowed to sell the drugs in the United States—something it could do before transferring the title overseas. The U.S. drug company deducted these so-called royalties from its U.S. income taxes, thereby reducing the amount of taxes owed. The IRS contested the royalty expenses because it did not believe that the Bermuda company had performed any services justifying the royalties. In other words, a U.S. company cannot just transfer or give away valuable assets to a related offshore company, especially when it is for the real purpose of making it appear that the company was paying rent on something it already owns.

The settlement for $2.3 billion is mind-boggling when you consider that the case only involved two prescription drugs.

The reason offshore schemes work is that tax haven countries do not charge much, if any, income tax on offshore transactions such as these. They are wooing U.S. dollars to their country to boost their economies.

Inter-Company Transfers

In 2006, the IRS also collected $3.4 billion in unpaid taxes from another pharmaceutical giant. The IRS contended that by making inter-company transactions regarding a few of its drugs' patents and trademarks, this drug company failed to pay proper taxes. In other words, the IRS alleged that the American company owned the patents to the prescription drugs and that the so-called transfer of ownership to a foreign company was a facade.

According to the IRS, the foreign company allegedly charged the American company huge royalties for the right to sell the two prescription drugs in the U.S. The American company then deducted the payments made to its offshore affiliated company from the billions of dollars in sales, thereby reducing the amount of income tax owed.

The IRS disregarded the technical structure of the company and alleged that the patent was really owned by the American entity, and argued that there was insufficient consideration to treat the paperwork as a legitimate arms-length transfer of ownership. The drug company denied liability, but still agreed to settle the allegations for over $3 billion. In dollars and cents, that's $3,000,000,000.00.

Rewards are Waiting for You

As exciting as these cases are, keep in mind there are many more out there like these.

For instance, two of these cases involved allegations of pharmaceutical companies concealing their ownership of four popular drugs. There are 4,000 other FDA-approved drugs out there. It is almost certain that similar schemes are going on right now. It's worth keeping your eyes open for them! In addition, offshore tax evasion is high on the radar of the IRS. For instance, in February 2009, Switzerland's largest bank (UBS) paid the IRS $780 million to settle allegations that it helped thousands of Americans hide bank accounts. It is an open invitation for you to report cases for a hefty reward.

Don't forget: The IRS Reward Program is not limited to tax evasion by companies, but applies equally to people who underpay taxes. For instance, one man made his millions in the stock market when telephone companies were deregulated. However, he was accused by the IRS of hiding his income and assets by setting up offshore companies in Panama and the British Virgin Islands. His companies purportedly generated over $500 million in revenue. He allegedly earned more than $125 million in 1998, but only claimed $67,939 on his federal income tax return and paid only a few hundred dollars in federal taxes. After the IRS accused him of tax evasion, a court ordered him to pay the IRS $23 million for back taxes.

Conclusion

These examples are just the tip of the iceberg. The IRS is inviting you to become an instant millionaire—or even a billionaire—by reporting those who do not pay their fair share. It is willing to split the recovery with you. This book is your roadmap for submitting a winning application.

Chapter Three

Beware of the "Other" IRS Reward Program

---

*The people will save their government,
if the government itself will allow them.*

— ABRAHAM LINCOLN (1809–1865)

Considering how many old laws are still on the books, it will not surprise you to learn that when Congress passed the law to create a new and improved IRS Reward Program (modeled on the DOJ Reward Program), it left the old, worn-out reward program intact. As a result, there are now two separate IRS Reward Programs—the one that never worked and the one that can pay you millions, if not billions, of dollars.

Convoluted? You bet. To make it worse, each of the programs have diametrically opposite rules, requirements, and rewards. So it matters greatly that you apply for the right one.

This is why it is absolutely essential that you scrupulously follow the strategies outlined in this book. In this way, you can meet both the technical and the unspoken requirements that will allow your reward to be governed by the new program.

A Law with Two Completely Different Faces

Although it is cumbersome to quote long passages from a statute in a book, the impact of the bifurcated statute is so important that it demands it. Below is the actual language from a seemingly simple law creating the new IRS Whistleblower Reward Program. What is not obvious, however, is that subpart (a) actually keeps the old program intact, while subpart (b) creates the new program.

> (a) In general. The Secretary, under regulations prescribed by the Secretary, is authorized to pay such sums as he deems necessary for (1) detecting underpayments of tax, or (2) detecting and bringing to trial and punishment persons guilty of violating the internal revenue laws or conniving at the same, in cases where such expenses are not otherwise provided for by law. Any amount payable under the preceding sentence shall be paid from the proceeds of amounts collected by reason of the information provided, and any amount so collected shall be available for such payments.

> (b) Awards to whistleblowers. (1) In general.—If the Secretary proceeds with any administrative or judicial action described in subsection (a) based on information brought to the Secretary's attention by an individual, such individual shall, subject to [limitations below], receive as an award at least 15% but not more than 30% of the collected proceeds (including penalties, interest, additions to tax, and additional amounts) resulting from the action (including any related actions) or from any settlement in response to such action. The determination of the amount of such award by the Whistleblower Office shall depend upon the extent to which the individual substantially contributed to such action.

(The full text of the statute is located in Appendix A. The cryptic formal IRS Guidance for the new program is found in Appendix B.)

It should be becoming clear that this chapter is not simply a history lesson, and it must not be skipped over because the new IRS Reward Program did not totally supersede the old IRS Reward Program, known as the Informant Program, or the "old program" for short. The Informant Program still exists and applies to reward applications which fall short of meeting the requirements of the new program.

Learning why the old program was a dismal failure will actually help you avoid making mistakes under the new program. Paying attention to what mattered to the IRS under the old program will also be useful in trying to glean what informal standards the IRS is likely to carry over into the new program. In other words, a little history lesson is more than just an interesting read; it affects how you put together your reward application and keeps you from making costly mistakes. Besides, if you fail to establish entitlement to a reward under the new program, the old governs your application and dictates how much (or, more likely, *how little*) of a reward you may receive, if any.

The Requirements of the Informant Program

In 1867, Congress gave the IRS the ability to pay rewards to whistleblowers, calling it the Informant Program. As we've said, however, the IRS did little to promote its new ability to pay rewards to people who provided information that led to payment of taxes and it chose not to pay out many rewards. The old program was fundamentally flawed. As a result, it was largely unused, unknown, and gathering dust.

The Informant Program still allows the IRS to pay a percentage of the amount of taxes, fines, and penalties collected from a person or company as a reward based on the information provided. For most of the duration of this old program, the maximum amount of a reward was $2 million. In 2004, the cap was upped to $10 million—which was too little and too late. However, most of the other oppressive conditions and requirements still remain.

The actual amount of a reward under the old program was based upon certain categories and the amount could not exceed the following percentage:

- 15% of what the IRS recovers for information directly leading to a monetary recovery.
- 10% of what the IRS recovers for information indirectly leading to a monetary recovery.
- 1% of what the IRS recovers for information that led to an IRS examination, but was not related to the amount collected.

Guess who decides if the information led directly to a recovery or was indirect? That's right, the IRS. And it did not even need to explain how it made its decisions.

Equally significant and troubling, the old program set maximum, but not minimum, rewards. The IRS did not have to pay a penny; it just could not exceed the maximum. Although it has proven to be a costly and short-sighted choice, the IRS opted to pay paltry rewards.

So, besides lack of popularity, the two biggest problems with the old program were:

(1) A maximum reward of $10 million.
(2) Unfettered discretion to the IRS to decide who and how much, if anything, to pay.

People with knowledge of large tax evasion schemes were unwilling to step forward for such a small reward. Because the IRS could pay only nominal amounts in any case (if it so chose), there was justified distrust as to whether real rewards would ever be paid.

For instance, if the IRS chose to pay a reward of 1% of what it recovered based upon a report by a whistleblower, there was nothing he could do about it. In fact, even today, the old program refuses to allow whistleblowers to have legal counsel to represent them during the process of submitting the claim or negotiating the amount of the reward. Without the assistance of counsel, individuals are vulnerable to being steamrolled by the IRS. There is no negotiating an amount of a reward and no explanation required. A letter simply arrives in the mail with either a small reward or a statement that no reward was granted.

In addition, the whistleblower could not appeal the amount of a reward to a court. It was "take it or leave it." Many whistleblowers tried to file suits to ask federal judges or courts to review the amount of rewards, but they were uniformly turned away. Because of the way the law was written, the courts lacked jurisdiction to review IRS informant cases. The language of the old statute gave complete and unreviewable discretion to the IRS.

Even within the government, the IRS has been notoriously secretive about its reward program and has rarely disclosed any details. In 2006 the Department of Treasury conducted an audit and released a formal audit report of the Informants Program. The results confirmed the suspicions.

As an initial matter, the 2006 audit only covered the last five years of the program (2001 through 2005), which one would think would be the best years or highest rewards. The numbers were shocking. So shocking that it motivated Congress to step in and revamp the reward program. Below is a chart of the amount of informant rewards paid over that five-year span:[3]

- Fiscal 2001 = $3.3 million
- Fiscal 2002 = $7.7 million
- Fiscal 2003 = $4.1 million
- Fiscal 2004 = $4.6 million
- Fiscal 2005 = $7.6 million

A quick glance at these numbers reveals that the IRS paid a total of only $27.3 million in rewards to all those reporting tax evasion during that five-year time period. For the 2005 fiscal year, the $7.6 million was split between 169 whistleblowers, for an average reward of just $45,000. The numbers were worse for 2003. The IRS paid out $4.1 million to 190 whistleblowers, for an average of $22,000.[4]

In total, for the five-year span, the IRS collected $340 million in taxes based upon information obtained through whistleblowers, but only paid $27 million in total rewards. That is a paltry 7.9% of what it recovered.

By paying such small rewards, the IRS was not encouraging citizens to help in catching tax cheats. In fact, it was methodically turning people away. Over the course of the old program, perhaps only one out of 100 who sought to tip off the IRS received even one of these paltry rewards. The majority of the time, the IRS did not even open an investigation to pursue the information.

The IRS Informant Program has not been successful and you *do not* want your case governed by it.

The New IRS Whistleblower Reward Program

Fortunately, when Congress overhauled the old, sagging IRS Reward Program, the changes were not merely cosmetic. They pack a punch. In the past, the IRS could give no more than 15% for any reward.

In the new program, Congress authorized the IRS to start paying rewards in the range of 15% to 30%. That means the *lowest amount* it can pay under the standard category is 15%—almost *double* the 7.9% average reward paid under the old program. You'll notice that Congress sweetened the pot here over the DOJ program (which set 15% to 25% for average cases and has only a limited category of cases eligible for up to 30% rewards) by setting the higher limit of a 30% reward for routine IRS cases.

Notice what a difference the new structure makes. Suppose Carrie works for a large bottling company and she knows that it transferred its secret formula to a related company located outside of the United States, and that company is charging fees to the American company for the right to sell the product; she could stand to earn hundreds of millions of dollars. Let's do some math. Assuming the IRS settles that case for $4 billion, Carrie could be paid up to 30% of that amount, or over $1 billion. Under the old program, she would have had to settle for a maximum reward of $10 million.

The old program set maximums. Today, by sharp contrast, the new program sets minimums. The new program does not have a $10 million cap. In fact, there is no maximum limit. With the right case, the reward could be in the billions.

Congress also required the IRS to open a new Whistleblower Office dedicated to paying whistleblower rewards. In other words, paying rewards could no longer be an afterthought, and treating whistleblowers as second-class citizens is no longer tolerated. To ensure that the program got off to a good start and maintained momentum, Congress commanded the IRS to annually report the progress and results of the Reward Program. No longer can it operate in secrecy.

The new program even allows you to bring in legal counsel. This is important for many reasons. An attorney can help you file the application and negotiate the exact reward amount with the IRS. Because the IRS can pay rewards between 15% and 30%, there is still a lot of room for the IRS to play games. Wouldn't you rather have 30% than 15%? Without strong negotiation, your reward could be cut in half. That's why it's beneficial to have legal counsel available to protect your rights. If necessary, an attorney can even appeal the amount of the reward to the U.S. Tax Court in Washington, D.C. Having a right to appeal and being able to ask a court to award a higher amount is a strong tool and should ensure you get a fair reward.

With the new program, whistleblowers have more options for negotiation. Suppose an attorney submits an application on Mark's behalf for a reward under the new program. He alleges that Acme Aces engaged in a certain scheme to evade paying $10 million in federal taxes. The IRS investigates and agrees. Acme Aces pays the IRS $12 million (which includes penalties and interest). The IRS must pay Mark a reward in an amount between $1.8 million and $3.6 million, depending on certain factors. If the IRS pays $2 million, Mark has the option of accepting that amount or asking the Tax Court to increase it to say $3 million, based upon the factors set in the statute.

As you can see, the new IRS Reward Program is embracing the use of a carrot to entice citizens to report tax evasion, rather than relying solely upon the big stick of the threat of a random audit.

Which Program Applies?

Although the details regarding the requirements of the new program will be thoroughly examined in later chapters, two key requirements are highlighted now because they dictate which program applies. If you meet all three, you are welcomed with open arms. Otherwise, your application gets bounced back into the old Informant Program.

First, the IRS will not pay a reward under the new program unless unpaid taxes, plus any interest and penalties collected, amount to $2 million.

Second, if the allegations are that an individual (as opposed to a corporation) failed to pay the correct amount of taxes, there is an additional requirement that the person's gross income exceeds $200,000 for at least one of the taxable years where the full amount of taxes were not paid. In other words, if you allege that your uncle Dale cheated on his taxes last year, you must show that he had at least $200,000 in gross income that year. This is in addition to the first requirement that the unpaid taxes total over $2 million. This is a safety valve to try to keep people from alleging tax evasion to get back at friends or neighbors with whom they had a fight, rather than helping the IRS recover significant underpayments.

If you meet both of these threshold dollar amounts, your application is governed by the new program with the higher reward percentages and all the other new features. If not, you guessed it; you are saddled with the old program.

Conclusion

The new IRS Reward Program has everything in place to be successful: a new, dedicated Whistleblower Office; annual oversight from Congress; minimums for amounts of rewards; and the ability for a whistleblower to use an attorney to negotiate with the IRS and contest the IRS's reward determinations. But beware! The old Informant Program still exists and you will be stuck there if you do not meet all of the strict requirements of the new program.

The remainder of this book focuses on the new IRS Reward Program, including how to meet the technical standards, plus how to assess your case and prepare an application capable of gaining the IRS's attention in order for you to receive a large reward.

Chapter Four

Examples of Domestic Tax Evasion Schemes Ripe for Rewards

Good people do not need laws to tell them to act responsibly,
while bad people will find a way around the laws.

— PLATO (427–347 B.C.)

Why are your odds of receiving a reward so good? Because the IRS collects $3 trillion a year! Thus, the IRS has estimated that underpayment of taxes is probably at least 15%, or $350 billion, in underpaid taxes every year. Therefore, the IRS could easily pay between $50 billion and $100 billion in rewards every year to citizens who report underpayment of taxes. Why shouldn't one of them be you?

This chapter outlines common domestic tax evasion schemes. It is filled with examples of the kind of conduct you could report to collect a reward. More schemes are included in the next chapter outlining foreign tax evasion, known commonly as offshore tax evasion. Do not assume you are limited to any of these examples, however. There are far more schemes than the ones listed in this book. And, since the number of ways people cheat on their taxes is only limited by their imaginations, new schemes are being devised every year.

It does not matter what scheme is used; a reward is available to you when you detail to the IRS how someone has underpaid taxes. In fact, you do not even need to prove fraud in most situations. If a person or company made an honest mistake by claiming a deduction they thought was allowable, but it turns out to be wrong, you can still receive a reward—as long as the IRS collects taxes based upon your application.

General Areas of Underpaid Taxes Ripe for Reporting

Let's start by listing general ways people cheat, followed by specific types of tax evasion. This will give you a good idea of how to spot tax evasion.

Here are some examples of the ways people and companies are cheating on taxes:

- Putting assets in another person's name
- Failing to keep or concealing records of income
- Making false entries into books and records or keeping two sets of books
- Paying by cash to avoid any written record of income
- Overstating deductions or claiming deductions that are bogus
- Lying about ownership of assets
- Mischaracterizing capital gains
- Embezzling funds or committing securities fraud (and not claiming it as income)

The key to successfully reporting tax evasion is to gather specific evidence to support detailed allegations that the person or company failed to pay the full amount of taxes owed, regardless of the reason why they underpaid taxes.

Generally, you need more than just a suspicion or even a slight admission from the person. For instance, if Mary brags at a party that she has come up with a scheme to conceal her business income and save $3 million in taxes, do not expect to receive a reward from the IRS. With such vague allegations, the IRS won't even open an investigation, much less take action. If asked by the IRS, Mary would simply respond, "Whatever do you mean? Can you tell me what taxes I owe for what?" The IRS agent would have egg on his face. He could not confront her with anything specific. He also lacks enough information to even try to get a subpoena authorized.

To receive a reward, what you need are details about Mary's business income and specifically how she concealed the income. Put yourself in the shoes of a busy IRS agent. Is there enough credible information that you, as the government agent, would contact Mary and demand payment of specific taxes owed? Do you have enough details to convince the agency to issue a subpoena?

In simple terms, you need to make your case so appealing that the agent wants to work on it. Then you must give him enough information that he can make a demand for unpaid taxes. The IRS wants to pay rewards. But it will do so only for specific and detailed information. Again, the type of tax evasion is not nearly as important as the quality of your information.

Let's consider a few additional types or categories of tax evasion. Several broad categories are discussed in more detail below to aid in your understanding of how to begin assessing potential underpayment of taxes. Many more have been placed in Appendix C.

Misclassification of Employees as Independent Contractors

Recently, the IRS began focusing on large companies improperly classifying employees as independent contractors. For example, in December 2007, after a lengthy investigation, the IRS asked a large company to pay over $300 million in purportedly unpaid taxes that should have been paid had the company treated workers as employees instead of independent contractors.[5] If you know of other large companies doing similar things, the potential rewards would be enormous.

The reason why companies sometimes fudge and treat those who should really be considered employees as independent contractors is simple: to pay less federal and state taxes. Any time an employer pays wages, it must withhold income tax, pay Social Security and Medicare taxes, and pay unemployment taxes. On the other hand, if they treat their employees as independent contractors, they do not have to withhold or pay taxes.

The company simply pays lump sum payments to so-called independent contractors. It is up to those individuals to pay all of these employment taxes themselves—at an increased rate from what they would pay as employees. The company does not pay taxes for independent contractors. For a variety of complex accounting reasons, the IRS gets short-changed if they really were employees disguised as independent contractors. Thus, what you need to know is that if a company has scores of employees but is pretending they are independent contractors, there is a potential tax evasion case to report.

Want more justification? Then think of it in another way. Reporting this type of underpayment of taxes also benefits the individuals forced to pay increased taxes as purported independent contractors.

You do not need to prove fraud. Even if the company has a decent argument that it had a good faith basis for such classification, if the IRS determines that they are employees, the company will have to pay back taxes. The whistleblower will receive a percentage as a reward.

The classification of employees versus independent contractors depends on the degree of control by the company and the amount of independence the person has to perform the work. The IRS uses a three-pronged analysis examining the behavioral, financial, and type of relationship factors.[6] The IRS will:

1. Examine what degree of behavioral control the company has regarding what the worker does—and how does he perform the work? For instance, if the person has to show up at the office at a set time, wear a certain uniform, and do tasks in a defined way, they are likely employees. Conversely, if they can work from home, and just ensure the work gets done, they may really be independent contractors.

2. Ask what financial control the company exerts, such as what expenses are reimbursed and what tools or supplies are furnished by the company. If the company supplies the truck and tools, the person is more likely an employee than if they are paid a fixed amount to get the work done in a manner they deem best using their own equipment.

3. Analyze what benefits the workers receive from the company that are normally given to employees, such as pension, insurance, and vacation. The IRS will try

to figure out whether they are really an employee receiving the normal benefits that employees receive.

Of course, there is no magical formula. Some of the factors may favor one answer and other factors another. The key is to examine the totality of the circumstances to determine whether the people really should be treated as employees.

The type of areas ripe for mistreatment of employees as independent contractors include:

- Construction
- Taxi
- Trucking
- Computer industry

If you know of another big company that may be improperly classifying employees as independent contractors, it is worth considering whether you can receive a reward for reporting it. For instance, the person who reported the misclassification to the IRS in the ongoing matter where the IRS is seeking over $300 million stands to obtain a reward of $100 million—assuming the IRS ultimately wins the case. There are many more instances like this waiting to be reported.

Abusive Trusts

When you die, you cannot take your property with you. By 2015, nearly $5 trillion in wealth will be passed on from one generation to the next. Using a trust rather than a will to transfer assets is becoming increasingly popular; in fact, the third most common filing of tax returns is by a trust entity, exceeded only by individuals, which is the most common, and corporate tax returns, the second most common.

The IRS has recently begun to crack down on the use of trusts to evade taxes. There are many ways trusts are being used to improperly evade taxes. A trust is not a magic wand that converts expenses into deductions. For instance, if an expense is not deductible—such as home heating or air conditioning—merely forming a trust will not transform it into an allowable expense. Those trying to claim unallowable deductions argue that the trust is a business and, therefore, electric bills are allowable business expenses. The IRS looks past such trusts and disallows such expenses. Thus, the person owes taxes once the improper deductions are removed.

Any time a person or entity forms a trust for the purpose of trying to deduct expenses which are not deductible to them as an individual, it is suspect. The key is examining whether the person has control over the trust. If yes, he must claim the income of the trust without deducting expenses that would not be allowed absent the trust.

Below are some examples of ways people try to use trusts to claim unallowable deductions or conceal income:

- Depreciating personal assets
- Deducting personal expenses
- Splitting income between multiple entities (frequently in multiple locations)
- Underreporting income
- Wiring or transferring income overseas and failing to report it
- Attempting to hide income or assets through foreign bank secrecy laws

Common characteristics of an abusive trust include either (1) hiding the true ownership of assets or income or (2) disguising the true nature or substance of transactions. They are treated as tax evasion or even fraud when the taxpayer, in fact, controls the trust, but makes it appear that he does not. That is because if a person controls a trust, he must claim the income from that trust on his annual tax return. The person who controls the trust cannot defer payment until the assets from the trust are distributed.

To disguise the improper nature of abusive trusts, a taxpayer frequently forms multiple trusts. By using layers of trusts, they hope to hide their true ownership interest. Sometimes they create horizontal trusts, with each one holding a different asset or type of asset. The goal is to make it appear that one person does not own all of the property.

More frequently, abusive trusts are vertical, meaning one trust owns or distributes income to another trust and that trust owns another trust and so on down the line. For instance, Steve owns a company valued at over $10 million, which produces $2 million in income per year. Steve does not want to pay annual taxes on the $2 million in income. Therefore, he forms a trust and places the assets of the company into it. He then forms a second trust to manage the assets. He forms a third trust to distribute the income. Each trust is built above the other to distance the true owner from the income. Steve hopes to delay paying taxes until he sells the business or perhaps never pay any taxes at all.

It is a lot harder for the IRS to figure out who receives income through a maze of trusts passing money between them than if Steve simply owned the company.

Of course, because Steve controls the trusts, by law, he must claim the $2 million as income each year. If you unravel the maze for the IRS and provide specific and detailed information about the trust, the IRS will pay a nice reward from the funds it collects from Steve.

The types of income or assets most commonly hidden through abusive trusts include rental agreements, contracts for services, and purchase and sale agreements. Basically, anything that involves distribution of income is ripe for an abusive trust by creating a series of trusts to conceal who really owns the assets or receives the income.

Promoters of Abusive Trusts

People often do not think of tax evasion schemes themselves. Rather, a person or company will advertise that they can help people reduce or eliminate taxes by forming trusts. They are often referred to as "promoters." Naturally, the promoter charges a fee for this information or for the service of actually setting up the trust. Those promoting abusive trusts charge clients anywhere from $5,000 to $70,000 to set up improper trusts.

If something sounds too good to be true, it is. You cannot avoid paying taxes on your income simply by forming a trust. The IRS will not allow you to hide behind the promises of a promoter, even if the promoter is an accountant or lawyer. If the IRS determines that it is an abusive trust, the taxpayer is liable for taxes owed, and possibly for fines and penalties, as well. The promoters can be liable too. One of the largest allegations of tax evasion involved the IRS going after both a large accounting firm and literally hundreds of individuals who followed their advice and set up the trusts.

Below are just a few examples from 2008, in which the IRS settled with those who helped create abusive tax schemes:

- The IRS recovered $17.2 million from a co-founder of a group that allegedly set up fraudulent trust packages and convinced clients not to report them as income.
- A banker pled guilty to helping a billionaire real estate developer evade income tax by helping him conceal $200 million in assets in Switzerland.
- The IRS accused a man of tax evasion who received more than $45 million from selling "wealth-building products" at offshore seminars he hosted in the U.S. The IRS alleged that he was selling bogus trusts for $1,250 and charging between $6,250 and $37,000 to attend his seminars. Not only did he allegedly help set up fraudulent schemes, but the IRS claims he did not report all of the fees from his seminars as income.

Recall that in 2009 the IRS also went after a large overseas bank for helping Americans hide money offshore.

As discussed in more detail later, the beauty of the IRS Reward Program is that a whistleblower does not need to prove that the tax-payer intended to cheat to receive a reward; if the IRS collects taxes based upon your report of an abusive trust, the reward is typically 15–30% of what the IRS receives. That is why the IRS was able to recover $4 billion for one scheme being promoted by accountants and lawyers; even if the person believed that the improper deductions were allowable, they still owed the taxes, and rewards were based upon funds recovered.

Conclusion

Don't be concerned if you do not see a particular domestic tax evasion scheme in this chapter or elsewhere in this book. The IRS Reward Program applies to *any and all* types of tax evasion, within the defined dollar amounts, provided you have substantial support and meet the technical requirements explained in the later chapters.

Chapter Five
Examples of Foreign Tax Evasion Schemes

There are dozens of foreign tax schemes and each is ripe for rewards. Some of the biggest tax cheaters are using offshore tax fraud schemes. The problem is that there is a Catch-22 when dealing with offshore tax evasion. On the one hand, it is more difficult to detect these schemes because the assets (or income) are hidden outside of the country. But on the other hand, these schemes almost always rise to the level of fraud. As explained in Chapter Eight, if you can show tax fraud, there is no statute of limitation. Therefore, you have some added time to unravel the scheme and gather information needed to earn you a sizeable reward.

After outlining the general types of offshore tax evasion schemes, this chapter will give you a closer look at a big ticket item—something capable of making you a billionaire. The rest of the chapter will present you with other examples of foreign tax evasion schemes. (Additional examples are also discussed in Appendix C.)

Regardless of the type of offshore tax evasion you report, there is no need to be disappointed because most would command rewards exceeding $1 million. That is because those who choose to commit this type of tax evasion or fraud often do so in large sums.

General Types of Offshore Tax Evasion

The ways people try to conceal income with offshore techniques or schemes are limitless. There are, however, a few common tactics. Below are a few examples of offshore tax evasion that qualify for rewards:

- Shifting income or pre-tax profits offshore
- Shifting or relocating assets offshore
- Failing to disclose third-party transactions
- Using offshore subsidiaries to lend money to a parent company
- Charging a related U.S. division royalty payments for assets shifted offshore
- Structuring records to make profits appear to be offshore
- Omitting income earned in a foreign stock exchange
- Omitting income earned overseas
- Omitting offshore gambling winnings

As mentioned earlier, you need more than just a suspicion to receive a reward. For instance, if Jim brags at a bar that he has won $6 million at an overseas Internet gambling website, do not expect the IRS to get excited. The IRS will not issue a subpoena to Jim asking for information about gambling earnings or bank statements based upon this type of limited information. Rather, you will need to have details about how or where he won the money and be able to direct the IRS to the location of the funds, such as bank account information.

Just as with domestic tax evasion, your reward depends upon whether you are able to gather specific and detailed information. Keep digging until you can describe the "who, what, where, when and how" of the tax evasion.

Keep reading the rest of this chapter to learn of many more ways people are evading taxes through offshore schemes. The potential reward that could be given for reporting these schemes could exceed a billion dollars.

Shifting Profits Offshore

One of the most common areas of tax evasion in terms of the sheer total of unpaid taxes is the improper shifting of profits offshore. As discussed in Chapter Two, the largest tax evasion cases pursued by the IRS involved allegations of offshore tax evasion, and in particular, shifting profits out of the country.

Any time a company devises a scheme whereby it appears that the profits of an American company are earned by an entity outside of the U.S., it is likely that tax evasion is occurring. Consider this hypothetical example.

A large U.S. bottling company, which we will call Suds Bottling, Inc., owns a popular soft drink which is sold nationwide. The value of the trademark and license is $5 billion. It sells franchises to thousands of companies, with each worth millions of dollars and paying tens-of-thousands of dollars a year in licensing fees. Suds Bottling transfers ownership of its trademark and licenses to a related offshore company located in the Cayman Islands, named Suds and More, Inc.

Suds and More gives Suds Bottling an exclusive license to sell soft drinks in the U.S. for an annual amount roughly equivalent to the income it receives from the franchise fees it receives. Thus, the U.S. company, Suds Bottling, reports no income on its tax return because it deducts as expenses the lease price charged from Suds and More. Suds and More reports on paper billions of dollars in profits. However, the Cayman Islands does not require it to pay taxes on sales outside of that country, and Suds and more does not pay U.S. taxes because foreign companies are not subject to the U.S. tax laws.

The key to the fraud is that an American entity cannot transfer assets offshore and then be charged back for using it in the U.S.

Assume that you work in the accounting department of Suds Bottling and are aware of the transfer of the trademark and licenses. You also know that your company is leasing the right to sell the popular soft drink in the U.S. You have access to documents that can detail the transfer to the offshore company and show that Suds and More did not pay fair market value for the trademark and licenses, i.e., that the offshore company did not pay $5 billion, but paid a nominal amount for bookkeeping purposes. You also know that Suds and

More does little real work, certainly not worth the $5 billion value of the trademark and license. You file an application for a reward, claiming Suds Bottling underpaid taxes.

In that setting, the IRS will likely open an investigation and vigorously pursue recovering the taxes. The IRS will argue that the transfer was a sham and disallow the American company from deducting the billions of dollars in lease fees it paid to the related offshore entity. In other words, the IRS will require the American company to treat the licensing and franchise fees as income and not deduct the so-called lease amounts paid to its affiliate.

The amount of taxes owed could easily exceed $1 billion. As the whistleblower, you would be eligible for at least 15%, or a minimum reward of $150 million, and as high as 30%, or $300 million. The amounts could be much higher depending upon how much the IRS recovers. There already have been multi-billion-dollar settlements with the IRS, and there are others out there.

As mentioned in Chapter Two, the IRS has gone after two pharmaceutical companies for allegedly shifting hundreds of millions in profits offshore for just a few popular drugs. Because there are 4,000 FDA approved drugs, it is likely that there are many instances of underpayment of taxes relating to patents for pharmaceutical drugs being transferred offshore. All it takes is for an insider to step forward.

Pharmaceutical companies are not the only ones thought to be engaging in offshore antics. Information Technology (IT) companies and other large companies may also be shifting profits offshore. The more common types of offshore profit shifting include transfers of ownership of the following types of assets:

- Patents
- Logos
- Manufacturing processes
- Intangible property rights, such as rights to franchises or secret formulas

Offshore tax evasion schemes are increasing and usually involve huge numbers. For instance, in 2008, the government estimated that more than $100 billion in taxes each year are lost due to offshore tax evasion alone.[7] The amount of taxes lost is actually far greater. Even based on conservative estimates, the IRS could be paying rewards of up to $30 billion a year just for offshore tax evasion.

Significant rewards are more than possible; they are likely. Offshore tax evasion has become one of the IRS's main areas of concentration. Given that those who commit offshore tax evasion are hiding large sums, this area presents the greatest opportunity for you to receive a mega-reward.

Accessing the Offshore Funds

Before reading further, you may be wondering if there really is that much offshore tax evasion going on. For instance, you may question how a person or company gets ready access to money being hidden or funneled overseas. After all, if the money is untouchable, there is little reason to hide assets in distant tax haven countries such as Switzerland or the Cayman Islands.

Gaining access to foreign funds is actually quite simple. The U.S. citizen or company opens a foreign bank account—most likely in a tax-haven country that does not report bank information to the U.S. government. The U.S. citizen then simply uses a debit or credit card from the foreign bank account, which is accepted in the U.S. just like any other bank card. Thus, a taxpayer can obtain cash or even pay everyday living expenses from the offshore funds.

Other methods of gaining access to funds overseas are more elaborate. For instance, the U.S. taxpayer establishes a foreign trust overseas and creates fake loans from the trust to the taxpayer. Of course, the loans are not repaid. Because loans are not taxable events, they are not reported to the IRS, making it hard for the IRS to detect fraud or unpaid taxes.

There are plenty of accountants who, for a fee, will help people open a foreign bank account or set up a foreign trust. They may even sell you an existing trust or tell you about a seminar on how to create offshore trusts. The fees for these seminars are often thousands of dollars. They can charge so much because of the large sums of money being rerouted into offshore accounts. For instance, if you worked for a tax accountant that makes up phony invoices for its clients, you are in a pretty good position to know that they are helping others cheat on taxes.

Helping Others Commit Offshore Tax Evasion

This raises another point worth addressing prior to identifying other offshore tax evasion schemes. What about those that help commit tax evasion? Are they liable?

The IRS is serious about going after those who help others evade their taxes. If a person knows they are helping another commit tax evasion, they are co-conspirators, and the IRS can go after them as well as the person who did not pay taxes.

The IRS has gone after large accounting firms and is willing to do much more, based upon credible reports of large-scale tax fraud. Recall that the IRS reached a settlement with an accounting firm that allegedly helped set up improper tax shelters offshore. The company settled for $456 million, which is in addition to the $4 billion the IRS collected from individual taxpayers who followed their advice.

Even Congress has entered the arena by publicly questioning the role of overseas banks in helping U.S. citizens dodge taxes. At just one offshore bank, which the IRS is now scrutinizing, American citizens hold 20,000 accounts containing $20 billion in assets.[8] How many of those account holders are cheating on taxes? How many others are hiding assets in other offshore banks? The IRS is asking you to help pinpoint which people are concealing assets and income offshore.

Before you put the cart before the horse, keep in mind, it's going to take more than just identifying a good suspect. If you search the Internet, you will quickly find out that there are plenty of people and companies out there offering seminars on "wealth retention." Many of these show their clients how to hide assets or income and promise to reveal secret tips for making assets invisible to the IRS. The government knows these companies are out there too, but it is not enough just to know that they exist. You cannot obtain an IRS reward simply by sending the IRS the website of a company that offers seminars that sound too good to be true. Even if you have attended the seminar and heard for yourself the promises of creating offshore bank accounts or trusts, you still may not have sufficient information for a reward—but you would be getting pretty close.

The key is you must provide specific evidence that taxes were actually underpaid. It is not illegal to form an offshore trust, but it is wrong not to report the income from it. So the fact that an offshore trust exists is not incriminating evidence. By the same token, you cannot simply tip off the IRS that a seminar is encouraging people to use such schemes. The IRS is not likely to issue subpoenas to those hosting or attending these seminars without evidence of active wrong-doing. You may need to show verifiable income was not reported by someone attending the seminar.

What you need is specific evidence sufficient to convince the IRS to conduct an audit and perhaps issue a subpoena. Remember, the IRS gets too many tips each year to try to track down every lead. The IRS is looking for tips accompanied by details they can follow-up on, such as names, places, amounts, and dates. Copies of an offshore trust document or a bank account number are examples of solid evidence. Of course, the mere existence of an offshore account is not enough. Again, it is not unlawful to have offshore accounts and many who have such accounts do properly report such income. However, it is a red flag because offshore accounts often accompany unpaid taxes.

Abusive Foreign Trust Schemes

Using foreign jurisdictions to hide assets is a major problem. It can be as simple as jumping on an airplane to sneak cash out of the country that was not claimed as income. In other words, a rich person interested in cheating on taxes may elect to hide a million dollars in an overseas bank. That way, they can still collect interest on the money without paying taxes. The IRS also won't even know to ask questions on how the money was earned. In addition, all U.S. banks automatically provide the IRS with details on interest paid on accounts, whereas some countries do not tell the U.S. how much it pays in interest on accounts. By sneaking funds out of the U.S., the IRS has no easy way of tracking funds.

More often, however, the foreign schemes are more elaborate, involving the formation of one or more trusts containing income-producing assets to give the appearance that such income was earned outside of the U.S. or earned by a foreign person or trust.

An offshore trust scheme usually starts off with the formation of a domestic trust or series of trusts layered upon each other. The trusts are used to make it appear that the taxpayer transferred assets into a trust that he does not control. Under the tax laws, income from a trust that you do not control is not ordinarily taxable to you.

However, in reality, the person forming a trust still wants to maintain ownership and control over the assets. They just don't want to pay taxes. Therefore, they transfer the assets from the domestic trust to a foreign trust set up in a tax haven country.

The key to evaluating whether a trust or series of trusts is improper is whether the funds, although flowing through one or more trust, are ultimately available to the original owner. When the original owner still has access to those funds, the income is taxable.

Conclusion

As you can see, there are more schemes than can realistically be included in this book. If you do not see a particular tax evasion scheme here (or in Appendix C), that is not important. Keep in mind that if a person or company is shifting assets or income offshore, it is likely they are doing so to improperly underpay taxes.

Assuming you have specific and detailed information, you are in a good position to make a preliminary judgment about whether it is proper or improper. Of course, you can ask an attorney to review your allegations in confidence and get his opinion on whether you have a claim worth filing. He can also help you gather more information and file the reward application.

You can also report an accounting firm that is helping others evade or underpay taxes, as long as you have specific instances of fraud and credible evidence to back up your allegation that it is taking place on a large scale.

If you know of a person or company that is concealing assets and income overseas, it can be well worth the effort to ferret out information. The largest tax evasion cases to date have involved foreign tax evasion. There will come a day when the IRS pays a billion dollar reward to the person who tips them off to such a scheme.

Chapter Six

Technical Requirements:
The "*Four F Factors*" of Eligibility

*Obstacles are those frightful things you see
when you take your eyes off your goal.*

— HENRY FORD (1863–1947)

A lthough the general concept of paying rewards for reporting tax-payers who failed to pay the full amount of their taxes is simple, the technical requirements of the new IRS Reward Program are not intuitive. Receiving a reward can actually be complex.

In other words, applying for and receiving a reward are two entirely different matters. If you want a realistic hope of receiving a meaningful reward, there are many strategic steps that must be followed.

This chapter addresses the technical requirements of the new program that must be scrupulously followed. Later chapters provide strategies and checklists for perfecting your application.

The "Four F Factors"

The new IRS Reward Program can be distilled into four key elements, which this book coins as the *"Four F Factors:"*

Filing first
Format is fundamentally correct
Federal tax funds unpaid
Funds are forfeited

If a single one of these *F Factors* is missing, your case may falter. That doesn't mean, of course, that having all *Four F Factors* will guarantee you a reward. The *Four F Factors* merely gives you a greater likelihood that the IRS will look favorably upon your case.

Getting the *Four F Factors* right will dramatically improve your odds of getting a reward.

The First Factor: Filing First

One day, while Rich was reading the newspaper over breakfast, he saw a press clipping that the company he worked for settled tax evasion charges with the IRS and paid $10 million. In the story, John Doe's attorney mentioned that his client is celebrating because the IRS gave him $2.5 million for reporting the underpayment of taxes.

Rich slapped his hand on his knee. "I knew about this! In fact, I knew a lot more about it than he did. I should've reported it!" Rich winced knowing that the $2.5 million reward could have been his.

Obviously, if you never file for a reward, you cannot recover one. But what happens when two people file for a reward relating to the same unpaid taxes?

The IRS Reward Program is so new that it has not yet sorted out this issue. In the related DOJ Reward Program, the answer to that question is clear, but the IRS Reward Program may ultimately take a different position.

Under the DOJ Reward Program, the government only pays a reward to the first person who properly files an application. The language of that reward statute clearly states a prior filing or submission bars all subsequent filings. This is known as "the first to file" rule.

The IRS statute, however, does not contain this same language. In fact, it is completely silent regarding whether or how to pay rewards when two people allege the same tax evasion. Although not conclusive, the IRS has provided some explanation in the form of an auxiliary document entitled IRS Guidance (which can be found in Appendix B). It deals with reward payments "proportional" to the value of information the whistleblower provides to the IRS in the application process. It is far from clear what this means. Will the IRS split rewards based upon level of information provided by the whistleblower, or will it follow the DOJ Reward Program model of paying only one person?

Because there is no "first to file" language limitation in the IRS statute, the IRS has not included a strict first to file rule. That means a person second to file may not be automatically excluded. Rather, the IRS may determine if there is any value added by the second filing in comparison to the first to file and thus pay a proportional reward amount.

Perhaps the IRS will choose to pay the second person to file a reduced reward if the allegations are substantially the same and perhaps offer no reward at all if there is no value added. However, if the second person brings new or more specific information, he may receive a sizeable reward. It remains to be seen whether the IRS pays multiple rewards or elects to adopt the DOJ approach of paying only one person per fraud scheme.

If the IRS does not adopt a first to file prohibitive rule, what about the person who is the first to file? Will their reward be reduced if the IRS pays multiple rewards? Presumably, the IRS will not want to pay more than 30% in total rewards for a single case. If the IRS pays rewards to multiple filers, will it still pay the first to file a minimum of 15%, as the statutory language seems to mandate, and then split the remaining available 15% with others who file? Only time will tell.

No matter how it all plays out, filing first is always the stronger position; so if you know of tax evasion and can satisfy the requirements, do not delay long before making your decision to file.

With that in mind, you must guard against the temptation of rushing the application process. Already, the IRS has publicly stated that 90% of the information it had received in years past from people who want to be whistleblowers has not been specific and credible. Under the new IRS Reward Program, the IRS demands that you do more than simply tip them off that tax evasion may be afoot. You must meet a higher standard and provide specific and credible information.

Racing to beat a hypothetical whistleblower from filing first can actually thwart your overall chance of receiving a reward. It will do you little good to be the first to file only to be rejected a year later when flaws in your application surface. It will hurt even more if you realize you could have corrected the deficiencies if you had taken more time.

If you are eager to get the process underway quickly while still producing a solid application, you should promptly contact a qualified legal counselor who specializes in whistleblower cases. He can help you prepare a quality application in a timely manner.

If history is any guide, your best defense in the first to file setting is not to speed up the process, but to slow down your mouth. Okay, before you think this is flippant, allow me to explain.

As a whistleblower starts contemplating the possibility of filing for a reward, he tends to start talking about it. He may even tell another person the whole fraudulent scheme in vivid detail. That is just human nature. Unfortunately, gossip travels fast. With potentially enormous rewards at stake, what is to prevent someone else from using your information to file an application and receive your reward?

More races to earn rewards are lost through a whistleblower's own loose lips than from someone else having the same notion. That is why it is important to fight the urge to tell others about your case and not to discuss the IRS Reward Program with anyone. More often than not, even if several people know about a given fraud, they haven't thought about reporting it or claiming a reward under the IRS Reward Program. If you begin thinking out loud about filing for a reward, you will plant that idea in their minds and potentially lose your reward.

The Second Factor: Format is Fundamentally Correct

Keep in mind that the reward statute provisions are very exacting. A single misstep in format can enable the IRS to reject your application.

Many people incorrectly think that they simply need to call the IRS hotline to be eligible for a reward. However, to qualify for the huge rewards available under the IRS Reward Program, you must submit a particular IRS form and follow other technical requirements that cannot be completed overnight.

IRS Form 211

The first technical requirement is that persons seeking a reward must fill out IRS Form 211. The form is available on the IRS website and at the end of this book in Appendix D.

Claims for rewards may not be submitted electronically or by fax. The only way to submit a completed Form 211 is by sending the original to the following address:

> Internal Revenue Service
> Whistleblower Office
> SE:WO
> 1111 Constitution Ave., N.W.
> Washington, D.C. 20224

You cannot hand-deliver the application. Not even your attorney can hand-deliver an application on behalf of a client. The IRS will likely refuse to accept it and he will be instructed to mail it.

It is also advisable to make and retain a copy of Form 211 and any attachments you include with your submission. The same holds true for any future correspondence. Keep a separate file relating to your reward application, including all correspondence with the IRS.

The IRS Guidance states that the IRS will provide you with a letter acknowledging that it received your application. Nevertheless, it is always a good practice to send your Form 211 via certified mail or another means requiring the signature of the recipient or other proof, in case there is ever an issue over when and whether your application was received. This would certainly be the case in a first to file setting when the IRS needs to determine who should get the bigger reward based upon when the application was filed.

It can take nearly one month for the IRS to process the application and provide you with an acknowledgement. For instance, one application was mailed via certified mail to the IRS on the 14th of the month. The IRS signed for it on the 17th at 2 p.m. The IRS listed it as being filed on the 18th of that month. The IRS sent an acknowledgement letter dated the 7th of the next month. It took three days for the applicant to receive the IRS letter. That totals 26 days from mailing the application to receiving a letter from the IRS acknowledging receipt of the application.

If you do not receive an acknowledgement within a month, contact the Whistleblower Office to make sure your application was not lost in the mail or misplaced. The process moves slowly at best. You do not want to incur further delays because your application was not processed.

Declaration: Certifying the Truth of the Allegations

You must also sign a declaration, which is a statement acknowledging you are making the statements under penalty of perjury, certifying that the factual information supporting your allegations is true. The IRS Form 211 contains the required declaration language, so when you sign the Form 211 application, you satisfy this requirement. There is no need to get the form notarized. Your signature is sufficient.

The declaration requirement is not designed to keep away good faith reports of tax evasion. It's another attempt by the IRS to keep people from using this program as a weapon in family disputes or to harass enemies simply out of spite and with no real goal of submitting a legitimate application. In other words, the IRS does not want to become embroiled in child custody disputes or other emotionally charged squabbles where the threat of reporting tax evasion is used as leverage. Of course, if you make up facts, the IRS could ask a criminal prosecutor to charge you with perjury.

Requiring a declaration also reduces the chances of someone using this program on mere impulse. People naturally take things more seriously and attempt to be more detailed and accurate when they sign a declaration under penalty of perjury. Remember, the IRS wants you to submit very specific and detailed applications.

The Third Factor: Federal Tax Funds Unpaid

The third *F Factor* is that the whistleblower must allege (and the IRS ultimately prove) that a taxpayer underpaid *federal* taxes. The IRS program is a federal program and applies only to federal taxes. It does not apply to state taxes. Very few states have tax reward programs, so do not be confused about what type of tax reward is available.

$2 Million Threshold Amount

As mentioned earlier, the new IRS Reward Program has a strict $2 million minimum monetary requirement. The IRS does, however, allow you to include interest and penalties owed together with unpaid taxes to reach that threshold.

This is a very important aspect of the new IRS Reward Program. It is also a significant change from the prior IRS Informant Program, which did not set a limit on the size of a case technically eligible for a reward, except that it would not pay rewards of less than $100.

Submitting a claim that does not meet this threshold dollar amount is probably the most common mistake made by applicants. Therefore, it bears repeating and restating:

> *To receive a reward under the new IRS Reward Program, the unpaid taxes you report must equal a minimum of $2 million (including applicable interest and penalties).*

If you want a reward under the new IRS Reward Program, you must meet the $2 million minimum. This restriction applies regardless of whether the alleged tax evasion is by a company or an individual taxpayer. Again, if you fall short of this amount, your application will be treated under the old Informant Program, with the lower percentages and no right of appeal.

This actually raises a curious issue. What if you allege that a person underpaid taxes by $2.5 million, but the IRS assesses the taxes or settles the case for an amount less than $2 million? Will you be governed by the new or old program? It matters because the old program limits you to a *maximum* of 15% and the new program guarantees a *minimum* of 15%.

Assume that the IRS settles the case for $1.75 million and gives you a reward of 7.5%, or $131,250. Can you appeal the decision? If the case is governed by the new program, yes. But the answer is no if it is governed by the old program.

In this example, your attorney should appeal to the Tax Court and argue that the new program applies because the amount of unpaid taxes plus interest and taxes exceeded $2 million. The new program does not state that the IRS must actually *collect* that amount, but that such amounts must be *owed*. The IRS is free to negotiate a case, but it cannot alter the statutory language.

The best case scenario would be that the court agrees that unpaid taxes plus penalties and interest is more than $2 million and the new program applies. Thus, you would be entitled to a minimum of 15%, and could ask the judge to set it at, let's say, 25% of the $1.75 million collected. If the judge agrees, you would receive $437,500, which is $300,000 more that offered by the IRS; an amount worth fighting for.

The Tax Court lacks authority to require the IRS to either open an investigation or settle a case for a certain amount. Therefore, in this hypothetical case, the court could not force the IRS to settle the matter for more than $1.75 million. But, it has authority to set the amount of the reward different than what the IRS is willing to pay. The court will set a reward amount between 15% and 30% that it determines to be fair based upon the standards in the statute.

Calculating the $2 Million Amount

There is an unexpected twist when it comes to computing the $2 million threshold figure. It refers to *the amount of unpaid taxes*—not *untaxed income or unjustified deductions*. Stated another way, when calculating the $2 million, it means there must have been an underpayment of taxes by $2 million (which can include any assessed penalties and interest). This is not the same as underreporting income by $2 million or overstating deductions by $2 million.

Here's how it works. Assume Edward filed a 2008 tax return and is in the 35% tax bracket because his taxable income was above $357,700. Leaving aside interest and penalties, in order for him to have underpaid taxes by at least $2 million, he would have had to understate his income by close to $5.9 million or overstate deductions by that amount or a combination of the two totaling $5.9 million. That is because the reward statute is based upon the amount of *unpaid taxes owed*, not the amount of income or deductions misstated.

Suppose Ed underreported income by $2 million, i.e., he failed to include $2 million in cash sales as income. He would have underpaid taxes by $700,000 ($2,000,000 x 0.35 tax rate = $700,000). Even with penalties and interest, it would fall far short of the $2 million in unpaid taxes for the new program to apply. Thus, your application would be treated as filed under the old IRS Informant Program.

By comparison, if Ed had understated income by $5.9 million—for example, by not reporting $5.9 million in offshore trust income—he would owe $2 million in taxes ($5,900,000 x 0.35 tax rate = $2.03 million). Even without interest or penalties, you would meet the $2 million threshold of the new program.

When you are on the lookout for tax evasion to report, look for a minimum of roughly $6 million in unreported income or overstated deductions (or a combination of the two). For instance, suppose Jill failed to report $3 million in cash sales and claimed $3 million in unallowable deductions, i.e., depreciation of her home and expenses relating to maintaining a second home. The total unpaid taxes in that scenario would be $2 million, based upon $6 million in incorrect income and deductions.

The good news is that the new IRS Reward Program allows you to aggregate amounts over tax years. For example, if Jill underreported income by $3 million two years in a row, you would meet the criteria because underreporting a total of $6 million in income translates into $2 million in unpaid taxes. It could even be $1 million a year for six years of improper expenses. (However, you must be mindful of the statute of limitation when determining which years you can add together. You will find a further explanation in Chapter Eight.)

Amazingly enough, people and companies really do lie or cheat by amounts over $6 million in improper deductions or unreported income. For instance, in 2008, the owner of a business listed tens of millions of dollars in personal expenses on the company books and now owes the IRS $70 million.

$200,000 Threshold for Individuals

The IRS statute contains *a second monetary threshold* requirement when the allegations of unpaid taxes relate to an individual, as opposed to a corporation. According to the IRS Guidance, if the one you alleged owes taxes is an individual, their gross income must exceed $200,000 for one of the taxable years at issue.

Simply stated, the IRS won't even look at your reward application when the taxpayer is an *individual* (single or married) and they did not earn a gross income of $200,000 in one of the years you contend they failed to pay the proper amount of taxes. For instance, if you allege that the person underreported $3 million in income last year and the same amount the year before, you must also allege (and the IRS verify) that the person also earned a gross income of at least $200,000 during one of the two years at issue.

An important point to keep in mind is that the $200,000 gross income requirement for individuals is *in addition to* the requirement that they owe at least $2 million in unpaid taxes. Don't make the mistake of thinking it is an "either/or" requirement. Because both are strict statutory requirements, the IRS cannot waive those dollar amount limitations.

The Fourth Factor: Funds are Forfeited

The last *F Factor* is often overlooked and yet it is crucial to your hopes of receiving a meaningful reward. Your reward is based upon the amount of funds forfeited by the person or company you are reporting. This means the amount the IRS actually collects.

The IRS cannot pay a reward until it actually collects the taxes owed and all appeal rights of the taxpayer have expired. Specifically, there must be a *final determination* of the taxpayer's liability, and the amount for which the taxpayer is liable must be collected by the IRS before you can be paid your reward.

The fact that the reward is paid out of money the IRS collects from the one you alleged owes taxes has several consequences. First, it could take a long time to receive a reward, especially if they contest that they owes taxes. It may even be five or six years before you see any benefit from your report.

Second, if the IRS does not open an investigation or recover any funds, you cannot receive any reward. Think of it this way, 15% of zero is zero. Thus, the major downside with the IRS Reward Program is that, no matter how good the case may appear on paper, if the government does not collect any funds from the delinquent taxpayer, you won't get a dime. And you have no ability to force the IRS to act or to try to collect the funds for the IRS yourself (as you do under the related DOJ Reward Program).

Suppose Gina files an application alleging that a company, which we will call Acme Aces, underpaid federal taxes by $10 million. After a fierce, three-year legal battle, the Tax Court ultimately issues a judgment for $15 million (which includes penalties and interest). Her reward seems certain. However, if Acme Aces files for bankruptcy and goes out of business without any assets left, her reward evaporates.

The reward is not based upon the amount owed, but the amount *actually collected*. Even with a tax judgment for $15 million, if the government cannot recover the money, Gina does not receive a reward. If, however, the company manages to pay $1 million, Gina's reward would be between 15% and 30% of that, i.e., between $150,000 and $300,000.

While it may seem like bankruptcy would be a huge hurdle, fortunately, it happens less than you may imagine. But it does happen. Therefore, part of your decision-making process in filing an application should include an evaluation of whether or not the person owing taxes has assets which the IRS could seize.

The point to remember is this: Even though your eligibility for a reward under the new program is based upon the amount of taxes owed, the actual amount of your reward must be based solely upon what the IRS *actually recovers*.

Conclusion

When you are evaluating whether you have a case worth filing for a reward, think in terms of the *Four F Factors* (Filing first; Format is fundamentally correct; Federal tax funds unpaid; and Funds are forfeited).

First, you do not want to delay in filing an application, as being the first to file is the only sure way to obtain a reward. Similarly, you do not want to tell others you are thinking filing for a huge reward, as they could race you to file the application. Second, do not rush the application process, because more people end up being ineligible for a reward based upon breaching a technical requirement than being second to report it. Third, you must show that the person or company actually underpaid taxes by $2 million, and if it is an individual, they must have had gross income of at least $200,000 during one of the years. Finally, your reward is a portion of the amount the IRS actually recovers. If you do not provide sufficient evidence of underpayment, or the person or company has no assets to pay the IRS, you will not likely receive a reward making it not worth your time.

It is worth the effort to fully understand the reward program and scrupulously follow every requirement, as outlined in this book.

Chapter Seven

Ranges of Rewards

What reward amount can you expect under the new IRS Reward Program?

It depends. But there are ways to make a pretty good guess. With the information in this chapter, you can estimate how much of a reward is possible—and even likely—assuming you meet all of the eligibility requirements.

Theoretically, the minimum reward for a tax evasion case against an individual is $300,000.00.

That is based upon the standard minimum reward of 15% and the threshold size of a case being $2 million in unpaid taxes ($2,000,000 x .15 = $300,000). Of course, there are a few nuances, so a reward could be smaller in certain limited circumstances. But there is no cap, ceiling, or maximum reward amount under the new program. Therefore, a reward exceeding $1 billion is possible, if not likely, depending on the case.

Three Levels of Rewards

The tax system in this country contains graduated tax levels with different percentages. Thus, there is little surprise that Congress and the IRS included levels of rewards with different percentages. This chapter explains those levels of rewards and provides insight into estimating under what range your potential case may fall.

There are three basic ranges of IRS rewards, each with their own criteria and exceptions.

Range One: 15% to 30%

The standard range of rewards under the new IRS Reward Program is straightforward. You receive at least 15%, but not more than 30%, of the total amount the IRS recovers, including taxes, interest, and penalties, which directly result from your application.

As explained in the previous chapter, the reward amount is based upon the total amount the IRS collects. The good news is that the IRS should base the reward upon any related action directly stemming from your information. For instance, suppose you allege that there is an industry-wide practice in which people in an association all use a similar tax scheme. If you can present specific and detailed proof against one of them and can name the rest, your reward will likely include the amounts the IRS recovers from all of them.

Consider this example. You file a reward application alleging that Rocky, the president of the company you work for, set up an improper offshore trust and evaded more than $2 million in taxes. You have specific and credible information, and the IRS opens an investigation. You tell the IRS how Rocky learned to do this from Sarah, a broker in a large stock exchange firm. During its investigation, the IRS is able to show that Sarah also promoted this scheme to five other people. The IRS collects $2 million from all six people, as well as $2 million from Sarah, totaling $14 million. The IRS should consider this as one related event and pay you between 15% and 30% of the $14 million.

The percentage of the reward you receive will be fixed by the IRS. To determine the actual amount of money you will receive, you simply multiply the total amount the IRS recovers from a taxpayer by the percentage of the reward. For example, if the IRS collects $2 million and sets the percentage at 30%, you will receive $600,000. However, if the IRS sets the percentage at 15%, you will collect $300,000.

As you can see, the exact percentage is very important. You can double your reward if you convince the IRS to pay 30%. This is why it can be very useful to hire a strong negotiator on your behalf.

The size of the case matters too. For instance, if the taxpayer cheated by $10 million, the lowest possible reward would be $1.5 million ($10,000,000 x .15 = $1.5 million) and the maximum would be $3 million ($10,000,000 x .30 = $3 million).

Below is a chart of ranges of rewards to give you some perspective:

Underpaid Tax	Range	Reward Ranges
$2 million	15–30%	$300,000 to $600,000
$5 million	15–30%	$750,000 to $1.5 million
$10 million	15–30%	$1.5 million to $3 million
$50 million	15–30%	$7.5 million to $15 million
$100 million	15–30%	$15 million to $30 million
$500 million	15–30%	$75 million to $150 million
$1 billion	15–30%	$150 million to $300 million
$5 billion	15–30%	$750 million to $1.5 billion

Guidance on Calculating Exact Percentages

How does the IRS select the percentage within the range? The reward statute allows the Whistleblower Office to make an initial determination based upon the extent the whistleblower "substantially contributed to such action." In other words, Congress has given the IRS some discretion in setting the exact percentage within the 15% to 30% range and the IRS evaluates several elements in determining the percentage. Of course, you still have the right to ask your attorney to argue how and why you substantially contributed, and, if necessary, appeal the amount to the Tax Court.

The IRS Guidance provides very little insight regarding how the IRS calculates the percentage. It simply states that the Whistleblower Office will make a final determination within the 15% to 30% range and that the exact amount will be paid "in proportion to the value of information furnished."

This means that the Whistleblower Office will judge the value of the information provided. Presumably, it will consider such questions as:

- How specific and detailed was the information provided?
- Did the whistleblower provide documents?
- How much help was the whistleblower during the interview?
- Did they provide names of credible witnesses to corroborate the allegations?
- Did the IRS have to basically piece together the case on its own?

Ultimately, the Whistleblower Office will be basing the percentage on how much you and your attorney contributed to the case. It is not entirely clear, however, what the value of your information is measured in proportion to. Is it the information provided by others, the information you provide, or the level of effort by the IRS agents? It will take time and perhaps a few court opinions before this language develops a uniform meaning. In the meantime, you and your attorney should be prepared to highlight your contributions.

Negotiating the Exact Percentage

What can you do to negotiate a higher reward?

The IRS actually has an incentive to negotiate with your attorney. This is because the program permits your attorney to appeal the amount of a reward to the Tax Court in Washington, D.C. From the time the IRS makes a determination of the percentage, your attorney has 30 days to file an appeal.

It is in the IRS's interest to avoid an appeal. So your attorney should maintain regular contact with the Whistleblower Office and invite it to discuss the reward amount prior to making a final determination. Your attorney can even submit a memorandum outlining the basis and reasoning for a certain percentage.

In some instances, the first time you may learn that the IRS collected taxes and assigned you a percentage for your reward is by letter from the Whistleblower Office. Even in that situation, you and your attorney still have an opportunity to negotiate with the IRS. Remember, you have 30 days to file an appeal. You should use that time to discuss the reward determination with the IRS. Don't delay.

Settlement discussions can take a few days or even weeks, depending upon the gap between the positions of the parties.

If you simply cannot agree with the IRS upon a fair reward, your attorney can still file an appeal to the appropriate court to set an amount. In essence, your attorney must file a formal legal proceeding in the U.S. Tax Court in Washington, D.C. If that does not spark an acceptable settlement, you will receive a mini-trial before the judge, complete with witnesses. The judge will make a ruling after reading the statute and Guidance and examining all facts and evidence presented by both sides.

There is a risk to filing an appeal, however. Regardless of what percentage the IRS letter may have awarded or offered in settlement discussions, they may ask the Tax Court to reward 15% if you file an appeal. In addition, settlement discussions are generally not admissible at trial, so you cannot tell the judge that they previously offered you 20%.

The IRS may also ask the court to downgrade the amount it stated in its letter. It can ask the court to rule that there has been public disclosure (as discussed in the next section) and argue that you are not entitled to any reward at all now.

This is why it is vital that your attorney knows the IRS Reward Program well, so he can protect your interests. He may be able to argue that the public disclosure bar does not apply or that you meet the original source exception. He will also need to present solid evidence as to why you should be awarded a higher amount within the range of rewards.

Because there is always risk in litigation, you could end up with a smaller reward. Therefore, you must carefully consider whether an appeal is in your best interest.

Factors the IRS Uses

When making a determination of the amount of a reward, the IRS must evaluate the significance of the information you provided, as well as any contribution made by you and your legal counsel throughout the process. Specifically, the determination of the reward amount is based upon "the extent to which the individual substantially contributed to such action."

This standard is hardly a picture of clarity, especially when the statute grants the IRS a fifteen-point spread between 15% and 30%. There seems to be a lot of room for the IRS to pluck out a number and argue that it reflects the contribution of the whistleblower.

How can you protect yourself from this vague standard being misused?

The related DOJ Reward Program initially contained similar vague language regarding setting percentages. Repeated requests from whistleblowers, however, prompted it to publish the guidelines it used. (A copy of the DOJ Guidelines can be found in Appendix G.) Even though they are merely analogous and not binding upon the IRS, they provide a good framework for your attorney to highlight the significance of your information and the role you and your attorney played in assisting the IRS.

Factors the DOJ Uses

The DOJ starts with the minimum amount of 15% and lists 14 factors that could increase that amount. It also lists 11 factors which may lower the amount toward 15% again.

Obviously, because of the differences between the programs, many of the DOJ factors do not apply to the IRS program. Still, many of the DOJ factors have been established through court cases. This means that judges have evaluated and ultimately accepted the arguments in support of these factors. Of course, these factors are not binding in an IRS case, but it is likely that the court's ruling on an IRS case will be guided by cases applying the DOJ program.

For that reason, your attorney should use any of the 14 factors that are pertinent to argue that a higher reward is warranted. For instance, an increase may be based on the detailed nature of the allegations and roadmap provided, the lack of prior IRS knowledge of the underpayment of taxes, and the risks you have taken in reporting tax evasion.

Be mindful that the IRS will also be likely to examine the 11 factors the DOJ would consider to lower the reward—such as, whether some aspects of the allegations were in the public domain; whether your knowledge was limited and general instead of specific and detailed; and whether you or your attorney provided much assistance to the

IRS after filing the application.

Planning for the arguments for the 14 factors and against the 11 factors from the start is vital, including how you will prepare your application and attached documentation in support.

Many of the factors focus upon your role and the efforts of your attorney in submitting the application and helping the IRS in its investigation. This is one of the few areas over which you have direct control and can act purposefully to increase your reward.

The Whistleblower Office will be thinking about how much help you provided when you first raised the allegations. Did you relay to the government extensive, first-hand details to better equip it to pursue the case? The IRS will also consider how much help you provided during the interview stage and beyond. Overall, were you a help or a hindrance to the IRS?

The activities of your attorney are equally important. Did he provide substantial assistance to the government? For instance, how well organized were the allegations? The less work it is for the IRS to understand and pursue your allegations, the more willing it will be to give you a larger reward. This is simply logical and fair.

In short, not only is your positive conduct a factor that can increase your reward, but any negative conduct is a distinct liability that can reduce your reward. In other words, if you are rude or make the IRS pull information from you, how do you think that will affect their decision when it comes time to set a percentage?

If you want to receive more than the minimum amount, you need to spend time doing the work to put together your best arguments and make the case as easy for the IRS to prosecute as possible. Be sure to highlight your efforts in bringing the tax evasion to light and make sure you mention every risk factor you can. Don't discount the sympathy factor of taking a great personal risk to right a wrong. If you are an insider, let the IRS know, too, that you are truly interested in ending an improper or fraudulent practice and seeing justice done.

Range Two: Less Substantial Contribution

Fighting to receive a higher percentage within the 15% to 30% category is not your only concern. If the IRS places you in "Range Two," the maximum reward drops drastically.

Range Two is essentially a reduced-fee category. The general Range One category does not apply if the whistleblower's application is principally based upon publicly disclosed information. This second range is known as a "less substantial contribution." It is modeled largely after the DOJ Reward Program's "public disclosure bar."

This reduced-fee category is based upon the notion that the IRS should not pay full reward amounts for information already in the public domain, which it could act upon without the help of a whistleblower.

The so-called public disclosure bar in the IRS program applies when the gist of your allegations that someone underpaid taxes is based principally upon information that has already been:

1. disclosed by the media
2. contained in a government report, hearing, audit, or investigation, or
3. revealed in a legal proceeding, whether criminal, civil, or administrative.

In short, a whistleblower is not eligible for the 15% to 30% range if his allegations of underpaid taxes are "based principally on" public information disseminated in one of the listed ways. Rather, he will receive between 0% and 10%. That is quite a drop!

The term "based principally on" is not a model of clarity. In fact, similar language in the 1986 version of the DOJ Reward Program has spurred numerous legal battles in the courts. The result is that the federal courts are divided over what it means.

The court decisions under the DOJ program vary greatly regarding what "based upon" means and generally fall into one of two camps. Some courts consider a matter based upon public information if the whistleblower's allegations are substantially the same as that in the public domain. Other courts find that allegations are based upon the public information only if the whistleblower knowingly derives his information from the publicly disclosed information.

It is too early to judge how this term will be construed by the IRS or the Tax Court. But, if you, as the whistleblower, can show that your submission was not based primarily upon public information, you have a good argument that this lower range of rewards should not apply.

The Amount of a Reward in Range Two

If you are stuck into Range Two, you are largely at the mercy of the IRS as to how much, if any, reward you will receive. The statute reads eerily like the old Informant Program, which allows the Whistleblower Office to award whatever it considers appropriate—but in no case more than 10%.

In other words, the IRS may—but is not required to—give a monetary reward at all. Equally discomforting is the fact that the range of rewards is so low: 0% to 10%. This is a throwback to the old days when the IRS had only a cap, but no minimum. In those instances, the whistleblower may receive nothing and could only receive a maximum of 10% of what the IRS collected.

Presumably, the IRS will decide the exact percentage in a similar manner as used for Range One, evaluating a combination of the quality of the information and the effort of you and your attorney. The more your information helps the IRS, the higher the reward. But, in this range, the maximum is 10%. Of course, your attorney still has a right to appeal the exact percentage. Therefore, if you are turned away or offered a small amount, say only 1%, it may be worth asking the Tax Court to bump it up to 5% or more.

Original Source Exception

The good news is that the IRS Reward Program has a built-in exception to the less substantial contribution range (aka public disclosure bar) for those with original source information. The truth is, Congress considered it too harsh to automatically downgrade every whistleblower simply because there existed some publicly disclosed information at the time a reward application was filed. Specifically, the "original source exception" provides that the public disclosure bar does not apply

> "where the information resulting in the initiation of the action ... was originally provided by the individual."

If you are wondering exactly what this means, you are in good company. The DOJ has been wrestling with similar wording in its DOJ Reward Program since 1986. In fact, one of the most litigated issues under the DOJ program is the meaning of the original source exception. In 2005, there was hope that the issue would be resolved when the U.S. Supreme Court reviewed a whistleblower case containing the original source exception.[9] Unfortunately, the Court failed to directly rule on the heart of the issue. Consequently, the lower courts remain deeply divided over what this exception means.

Here is one example of how the exception works. Suppose you contact a state agency alleging that certain conduct is wrong before filing for a reward application. The agency takes some administrative action against the taxpayer based upon your report. That administrative action is a public disclosure, just as much as a newspaper article. You then file for an IRS reward. Even though the public disclosure bar would be triggered, you would meet the original source exception because you were the catalyst for the public disclosure.

Because of the complex nature of the public disclosure bar and original source exception and the drastic effect on a potential reward, if this is a potential issue in your case, you will need to enlist an experienced attorney familiar with these legal principles.

Range Three: Reduction for those Planning the Fraud

The IRS statute contains a third range or category of rewards. Range Three is a reduced reward range for whistleblowers who have played a big part in the tax fraud they are reporting. Before your blood pressure rises over the thought of someone being rewarded for cheating, this category is specifically designed to separate those who have initiated fraud from an employee who was just following orders.

As an initial matter, when the person reporting the case actually came up with the plan to evade taxes or has been criminally convicted for tax fraud in the matter, the IRS may outright deny a reward. The statute also provides that the IRS may greatly reduce the amount of a reward if the claim is brought by an individual "who planned and initiated the actions that led to the underpayment of tax." In that situation, the statute leaves wide discretion for the IRS to weigh just how much of a principal actor you were and reduce the reward accordingly, down to zero if it really was your idea and you helped set it up.

This provision makes sense. If you are an accountant and you sell a client an offshore trust kit to help them improperly evade taxes, you should not be able to turn around and get a full reward for reporting them. However, the statute leaves room for situations where a reward may still be in store for those who aided the tax fraud. For instance, perhaps your boss came into your office and said, "Please help me brainstorm how to cheat on my taxes." If you engaged in a short conversation, but then had second thoughts about actually setting up the fraud, the IRS may still give you a significant reward.

Of course, if you are the architect of a tax fraud scheme, you may have other concerns, such as whether you have some criminal exposure. Frequently, a person that had a hand in the initiation of the fraud hires legal counsel and approaches the criminal prosecutors seeking indemnity before filing for a reward.

Be mindful, however, that Range Three does not apply to employees who were asked to carry out tax evasion. For instance, if the owner of a company sets up an abusive trust in the Cayman Islands and you, as the bookkeeper, mailed checks to the bank, you are not governed by Range Three. In fact, you would be a perfect whistleblower and receive the highest reward for stepping forward. You did not plan the fraud, but have inside information as to how it works. Who knows, you may even get close to 30% with that type of direct information about offshore bank accounts.

The bottom line is that mere participation in the scheme is not what this provision is addressing. It applies to those who *initiated* it.

Finally, the statute makes it clear: if you are convicted of the crime of tax evasion, you cannot get a reward for reporting it, not that anyone in their right mind would even try filing for a reward in those situations. Losing out on the chance to obtain a sliding scale range of a reward is not what you should be thinking about. Rather, you may want to consider: how do you look in stripes? Seriously, do not take the chance. Keep far away from committing tax fraud.

Conclusion

There are three different categories or ranges of rewards, and it is important to ensure you end up in the right one. In addition, each category also has a wide range of rewards determined on a sliding scale. You should, however, have a role in negotiating the exact amount of the reward, and have a right to appeal a low reward to the Tax Court.

Chapter Eight
Restrictions and Limitations

If I had permitted my failures, or what seemed to me at the time a lack of success, to discourage me, I cannot see any way in which I would ever have made progress.

— CALVIN COOLIDGE (1872–1933)

There are a few restrictions and limitations to the new IRS Reward Program, ranging from prohibitions of certain classes of informants to stale claims. In fact, the IRS statute itself lists eight specific reasons why the IRS may not even process your reward application. This chapter outlines and discusses the two primary limitations on types of claims that are not eligible for a reward. The next chapter addresses the six categories of restrictions on who can apply for rewards. Any one of these eight restrictions can disqualify your application.

The first and most common limitation relates primarily to the specifics—or, more precisely, the lack of specifics—of the allegations. The IRS broadcasts that it reserves the right to outright reject applications that are so poorly written that they do not even allege the threshold requirements.

Under the second limitation, the IRS also systematically rejects claims barred by the statute of limitation. Understanding these two key restrictions can make the difference between whether you have a "diamond in the rough" that can be cleaned and polished into a winning application or whether you are wasting your time with a hopeless lump of coal.

Claims Lacking Merit

The IRS statute states that the agency need not process claims that, on the face of the application, either lack merit or "lack sufficient specific and credible information." In other words, if the IRS can tell from a quick read that your submission lacks merit, it does not need to expend any effort on it. The government internally refers to these as "dog" cases. Nobody wants to spend effort working on a case that clearly lacks merit.

Although the IRS Guidance provides that the IRS has discretion to return Form 211 to the whistleblower to add more details, don't count on it. A busy IRS agent doesn't have time to send it back or try to make sense out of your case or fill in missing information for you. Rather, a rejection letter will one day show up if your claim fails to meet the requirements or is too vague or confusing to be worth the time to open an investigation.

Statute of Limitation

The most significant restriction or limitation on filing claims is the statute of limitation (SOL). A SOL is a law setting the deadline or a maximum period of time within which a lawsuit or claim may be filed. If it is not brought within that time period, the other person does not need to pay.

You are probably familiar with a statute of limitation for bringing a lawsuit against someone who negligently causes a car accident, for instance. The time limitation to bring a suit varies greatly between states, ranging from two to six years. In fact, states have different SOL for different actions. For breach of contract claims, the SOL can be one year or six years. The key is that if you do not file suit within the SOL, you lose your rights forever.

The importance of the SOL cannot be overstated. It directly affects the ability of the IRS to pay rewards. If the IRS cannot recover unpaid taxes, it cannot pay you a reward. Again, 15% of zero dollars collected by the IRS equals zero reward.

The IRS has its own SOL. In fact, it has three different periods of statute of limitation for different types of unpaid taxes, consisting of three years for most underpayments of taxes, six years for a few important exceptions, and no statute of limitation at all if the IRS can prove fraud. This chapter explores all three ranges.

Three-Year Statute of Limitation

Generally, there is a three-year statute of limitation for the IRS auditing a tax return. The audit is a prerequisite to determining the amount of unpaid taxes. Unless the IRS can demonstrate that a regulation containing a longer SOL applies, the default is that the SOL is three years.

In general, the SOL begins to run from the later of these two dates:

(1) the due date of the tax return (even if the IRS grants an extension), or

(2) the date the tax return is filed.

Knowing the moment or date that the three-year SOL starts to run helps you determine when it expires. The first date listed above generally is the date that all taxes are due, April 15, following the end of the tax year at issue. The second date only applies if the tax payer files late. Those are the start dates for the SOL. The IRS would need to initiate an audit within three years from that time.

In sum, if you cannot meet one of the two following SOL periods discussed below, then the SOL is three years.

Six-Year Statute of Limitation

If your allegations are beyond three years, do not despair just yet. There are two major exceptions to the standard three-year SOL. The first one applies when a person significantly underpays certain types of taxes. It has very technical requirements and you must specifically fit within the definition for the SOL to be six years.

▶ **Underreporting Income by 25%.** The IRS applies a six-year SOL when the person underreports a significant amount of income on their tax return. The IRS uses a complicated way of saying this, namely that the taxpayer must have omitted from gross income an amount exceeding 25%. Basically, if a person or company underreports their gross income by 25%, the IRS gets longer to conduct an audit. Six years, in fact.

The term "gross income" generally means the taxpayer's total or gross taxable receipts during the year from all sources. In other words, it includes salaries, income from the sale of stocks, and income earned on trusts that you control.

Consider this example. Matt owns his own company. He places $10 million in a trust. His accountant tells him that the income on the trust is not taxable. The accountant turns out to be wrong. The trust has earned $1 million a year in income for the past 10 years. Assume Matt had a gross income of $2 million a year, excluding the trust.

In the tenth year, the IRS claims that Matt should have reported the trust as income. It is allowed to open an audit for the past six years because the amount of income not reported in each year was more than 25% of the amount of income he did report. (In other words, the unreported income of $1 million is 50% of the amount of income he did report. Therefore, the SOL is six years.) The IRS, however, will not be able to recover the full ten years of unpaid taxes because the SOL is six years.

The IRS follows the same process and applies the same six-year SOL to businesses. The only difference is how it defines the term gross income. For a business, it means the total of the amounts received or accrued from the sale of goods or services (if such amounts are required to be shown on the return) prior to diminution by the cost of such sales or services.

Clear enough? Well, it covers just about any type of income that would normally be included in income on a tax return. This is before a company may deduct allowable expenses. Again, it is gross income, not taxable income, that must be included on the tax form.

Finally, it does not matter whether the omissions by the taxpayer were innocent mistakes. Because of their significant size and the extra time it may require the IRS to assess a "deficiency," the IRS is allowed six years to conduct an audit for all such tax returns. That means you have six years to file a claim (leaving time for the IRS to act) if you are alleging that the person or company underreported income by 25%.

➤ **Underreporting Excise Tax by 25%.** The second area where the SOL is six years is where there has been an omission of more than 25% of excise taxes. If a taxpayer underreports the amount of excise taxes owed by 25%, you can receive a reward for unpaid excise taxes going back six years. For instance, if they owed $5 million in excise taxes, but only reported $3 million, they still owe the IRS $2 million in excise taxes.

To calculate the 25% omission, start with the amount of excise taxes owed ($5 million) multiplied by 0.25. This equals $1.25 million. Here, the entity underreported $2 million, which is more than $1.25, or 25%.

However, the six-year statute of limitation will not apply in situations where disclosure of the item giving rise to the excise tax was made in a manner that adequately lets the IRS know of the existence and nature of the dispute. In other words, if the IRS already knows of an issue regarding how the excise tax was computed, it cannot wait for six years to begin auditing. For instance, the taxpayer may be contesting that the IRS's method of calculating excise taxes is wrong. If the IRS knows of the dispute, it cannot rely upon the six-year SOL.

No Statute of Limitation

There is no SOL for tax fraud. That is right. The IRS can always recover unpaid taxes when there is misconduct rising to the level of fraud.

The IRS rules state that there is no statute of limitation for:

- Filing a false or fraudulent return,
- Willfully attempting to evade tax, or
- Failing to file a return.

In each of these instances, the tax may be assessed or collected at any time, even 10 or more years later.

In the hypothetical case of Matt, the IRS could not recover the underpaid taxes that were seven to ten years old. However, if the facts are changed slightly and you knew that he was cheating, there is no SOL. For instance, if Matt's accountant told him that the income was taxable and he chose not to report it, that would be fraud. The IRS would be able to go back the ten years or even longer if it desires.

The same is true for the excise tax hypothetical. If an entity lies about excise taxes owed, that is fraud and there is no statute of limitation. You could go back a dozen years or more.

However, before you get too excited, you still must convince the IRS to take an old case. The IRS is cautious about taking older cases, because these cases require the IRS to prove, to the satisfaction of a court, that the person or company knew that it was committing tax fraud.

If a person or company had a reasonable belief that they did not owe taxes or that a deduction was allowable, that is not fraud. Typically, a person who owes millions of dollars in taxes hires accountants and lawyers. Generally, if a tax attorney sends a letter to a client stating that they have a reasonable basis for not claiming income, the taxes will still have to be paid, but nonpayment will not be treated as fraud.

Of course, simply obtaining a letter from an attorney or accountant is not an absolute shield. If you can show that the person obtaining a letter from an accounting firm or attorney knew that it was not worth the paper it was written on, there is no reasonable reliance. Therefore, if you know that the taxpayer has a letter on file claiming that the accountant stated that certain income was not taxable, you need to include in your reward application why the person did not rely upon it. For instance, they may have told you over drinks that they have a sweet deal with the accountant who writes letters for cash or some other admission that they knew that the letter was not valid and they knew they were cheating.

Courts have also added the requirement that for tax fraud, the IRS must prove that the taxpayer had guilty knowledge by "clear and convincing evidence," which is a high burden. Normally, the burden in a civil case is the "preponderance of evidence," which means that something is more likely than not. The clear and convincing standard for fraud approaches that of a criminal case, which requires a showing of evidence "beyond a reasonable doubt."

If part of your proof of tax fraud is that the person told you they were cheating, that would help push you into the clear and convincing evidence standard. Of course, if all you have is your word against theirs, the IRS may not even take the case. Remember, documents or other tangible evidence is the best way to make a solid case. Emails containing admissions are also excellent proof. In fact, without this type of proof, it will be hard to convince the IRS to take on a case where they must prove intent to defraud.

In addition, the IRS faces difficulties in proving old tax fraud cases because the evidence may have been lost or destroyed. Therefore, it is hard to get the IRS excited about taxes that were unpaid ten years ago unless you have a smoking gun document or some credible admission by the taxpayer that they were cheating.

➤ No Requirement to Amend a Return

Assume for the moment that a person underpays $10 million in taxes, but the standard SOL has expired. Other than proving fraud, is there some other way to get around the SOL? For instance, doesn't the person have a duty to file an accurate tax return, so they are required to file an amended return? Some people have argued that the SOL should not begin to run until the taxpayer files a correct or amended tax return. Unfortunately, the courts disagree.

As an initial matter, there is no duty to file an amended tax return. Of course, a person may file an amended return, but they do not need to, even if the initial filing was completely wrong.

Assume that Thomas files a tax return which does not claim $6 million in income from a foreign trust. The SOL begins to run the later of when the tax filing was due (April 15) or when it was actually filed. Assume that he filed on April 15 of 2005. The standard three-year SOL would expire on April 15, 2008. If, however, Thomas underreported income by more than 25% of his gross income, the SOL would be six years, or April 15, 2011.

Let's change the facts slightly. Assume that Thomas filed an amended tax return on November 30, 2005, which amended the one filed on April 15, 2005. He still did not report the trust income, but added some allowable business deductions he had not included in the original tax return. Would the SOL be extended to November 30, instead of April 15? No. The courts have consistently ruled that because there is no duty to file an amended return, the SOL start date is not restarted by any amended return.

In 1984, the U.S. Supreme Court held that the filing of an amended return does not restart the running of the three-year statute of limitation, provided of course that the amended filing was not fraudulent (which, in that case, would not have a statute of limitation).[10] The Court also confirmed that there is no duty to amend a tax return.

This means that you cannot argue that because the original tax return had an error in it (but was not fraudulent), the SOL should not start until an amended return is filed stating the true amount of taxes owed. That is because there is no duty of a taxpayer to file an amended return. The IRS code permits, but does not require, a taxpayer to file an amended return.

Of course, if you can prove that the original tax filing was fraudulent, there is no SOL. Thus, there is no need to worry about an amendment. But, it is important to know when the SOL starts and stops so you do not waste time pursuing old cases. Remember also that to prove tax fraud you may need the equivalent to a smoking gun document.

Conclusion

The two biggest reasons why reward claims are rejected are (1) you lack sufficient information, or (2) the allegations are old or stale. If you do not have specific and detailed information based upon credible information or documents, you have a slim chance of being paid a reward. In addition, if your allegations are outside the statute of limitation (SOL), you cannot receive a reward, period. If the IRS can prove that the person committed fraud, i.e. intended to cheat on taxes, there is no SOL.

There are just two SOL periods. The main SOL period is three years and covers almost every case. The exception is the cases that fall under the narrow six-year SOL—which applies when a taxpayer underreports their gross income or excise taxes by at least 25%.

Chapter Nine

Who Can Apply? Entrepreneurs and Insiders

Ambition must be made to counteract ambition.

— James Madison (1751–1836)

Who can apply for a reward? Is it limited to insiders who know the inner workings of a company first-hand? Can a friend, coworker, or simply a tax-reward entrepreneur file an application?

Insiders working for a company and learning of tax evasion in the course of their jobs as well as those snooping around for tax evasion are equally welcome to submit a claim for a reward.

There are only very few limitations as to who can apply for an IRS reward. This chapter describes the small handful of restrictions. It also addresses special issues affecting entrepreneurs as whistleblowers.

Filings by Insiders are Ideal

Let's begin with who makes the best whistleblower. The short answer is an insider, someone with direct and personal knowledge of the facts and events supporting the allegation that a taxpayer has underpaid taxes.

Why does the IRS love insiders? They know where the bodies are buried and can tell the IRS where to look. An insider often knows bank account information, specific income that was earned but not claimed, or deductions that are bogus. The IRS frequently needs more help with proving intent than it does sorting out whether a particular item constitutes taxable income or an allowable deduction. The IRS knows the regulations but will need help to identify specific income or deductions to examine.

A bookkeeper who mails checks to offshore bank accounts or a business partner who knows the affairs of the company are just two examples of insiders. Of course, an insider includes pretty much anyone who has directly looked at the actual documents at issue, such as phony invoices or abusive trust documents.

There are very few obstacles for an insider in claiming a reward. The only issues that may occur would be if you were to wait so long to file the application that the allegations have either been barred by the statute of limitation or become public knowledge. If they become public before you apply, you would face issues regarding whether the public disclosure bar applies or whether you would meet the original source exception. Of course, it may still be advisable to file claims in the face of a public disclosure—if you can meet the original source exception or have information that the IRS needs to prove its case. If you meet the original source exception, you may still fall into the 15% to 30% category. Even if you cannot meet the original source exception, you may still receive a healthy reward of up to 10%, depending on what information you can offer the IRS.

Entrepreneurs are Welcome

The IRS has not closed the door upon entrepreneurs, but welcomes them. In general, entrepreneurs are defined as people willing to take upon themselves a new venture or enterprise, while accepting full responsibility for the outcome. In the case of whistleblower rewards, an entrepreneur is a person who ferrets out tax evasion and reports it to obtain a reward. They are modern day bounty hunters.

While the IRS does not discourage entrepreneurs, there are some limits that affect them.

First, and foremost, it is difficult to acquire the necessary information as an outsider. Since only applications that contain detailed and specific information are likely to result in the IRS opening an investigation, let alone a recovery by the IRS, the odds are against an entrepreneur.

This leads to the heart of the question: Can you, as an entrepreneur, gather enough information to entice the assigned IRS agent to open and vigorously pursue your tax evasion allegation?

As discussed earlier, IRS Form 211 asks you to provide "a detailed explanation and all supporting information in your possession and describe the availability and location of any additional supporting information not in your possession." What information do you have on this point?

The IRS also asks how you learned of the information and your relationship to the taxpayer. In other words, the IRS will take a preliminary look at your application to determine whether it is even worth opening an investigation. You need to be honest. Tell the IRS that you gathered your information from searching land records, for instance, or whatever you did to piece together your evidence of tax evasion.

The IRS will not automatically reject your claim because you are an entrepreneur, but it will raise a few questions. The IRS agents may wonder if you are just relying upon a hunch or if you really have a winning hand, based upon specific and detailed facts. You must quench these doubts right away by preparing a very detailed application with a roadmap and full description of how and what amount of taxes were underpaid. Showing yourself to be a thorough, well-prepared professional who understands what is at stake will increase your credibility with the IRS agents.

Another potential impediment to entrepreneurs is that they often lack information regarding the intent of a taxpayer. Although intent is not required for most matters, fraud is still the fabric that makes for the best reward applications. Showing that a person intended to cheat is also vital to ensure that there is no statute of limitation (should your allegations fall outside of the statute of limitation periods otherwise).

How to Get Started

One of the best ways for an entrepreneur to get started is to focus upon a known tax evasion scheme. For instance, if you read a newspaper article about a tax fraud matter in a different city than where you live, you can find out whether the same scheme exists where you live or in other places where you have access to information.

Of course, this raises the question of whether alleging that a similar company doing the same thing as disclosed in the media is considered a public disclosure? It all depends.

Consider this example. Suppose you read in your local newspaper in Minnesota that John Doe in Indiana has formed an improper lease strip where an accounting split assigns the lease income to a person overseas, while retaining only the expenses to the property himself. In other words, John Doe claims the expenses for the asset but not the income. A newspaper described the scheme in sufficient detail that you realize your boss, Debbie, is doing exactly the same thing.

Ask yourself, would an IRS agent reading the same newspaper article automatically know that Karen in Virginia is doing the same thing? If the answer is yes, the public disclosure bar applies. If it's no, the bar should not apply.

In this hypothetical, the answer is no. So it would be perfectly okay for you to file an application.

If this were not the case, then simply reading this book would bar every reader from filing applications on any of the tax schemes mentioned here.

Ways to be an Effective Entrepreneur

If you are an entrepreneur, you can increase your odds of obtaining a reward. As already mentioned, you need to follow the strategies in later chapters on putting together an application capable of gaining the attention of the IRS.

Hiring legal counsel is another option. An attorney can give you an honest appraisal of your allegations and, if he accepts the case, this may also lend you greater credibility with the IRS.

The age of your allegations is also a big factor. If you allege a taxpayer underpaid taxes within the statute of limitation (SOL) periods, you are in pretty good shape. Again, for claims within the SOL, there is no requirement to prove fraud. However, if some or all of your claims are outside of the SOL and you need to rely upon proving fraud, you will face a big hurdle. It will be very difficult for you as an entrepreneur to show that the taxpayer intended to cheat because your information is second hand. The IRS would prefer an admission or smoking gun document to prove fraud. This may not be possible for you.

There may be times where the fraud is so obvious that the facts speak for themselves. For example, if a person used a fictitious name or a dummy company, the intent is clear. However, without that, a busy IRS agent may not be willing to spend months or years trying to prove fraud, if you bring no compelling inside information to the table.

If you must prove fraud, make an honest appraisal of your case. Ask yourself, would a government attorney be able to stand before a judge and convince them that the person knew they were cheating?

Public Disclosure Bar

Perhaps the biggest obstacle for an entrepreneur is the public disclosure bar. This concept was introduced in Chapter Eight. Basically, if the tax evasion scheme is already in the public domain, the IRS can limit your reward to between 0% and 10%, unless you are an original source of the information.

It is unclear how the IRS will define an original source. The answer may rely on the source more than on how or where you got your information. It makes a difference. For instance, if you read a news story that Frank has been hiding assets in the Cayman Islands and then do some digging to verify the news account, you likely will be subject to the public disclosure bar.

Conversely, you have a much better chance of a reward if you simply pieced together information yourself from public sources and are the one who is first painting the picture of tax evasion. Perhaps you deduced the tax evasion after retrieving some information from a company website and other information from land records, but there was no public allegation that the person or company underpaid taxes.

In short, if you are the first one to figure out that it amounts to underpaid taxes, you have a good argument that you are an original source. But the IRS may still not agree and may ask whether you are the one who triggered the public disclosure. This is an area of much debate in the related DOJ Reward Program. Of course, the safest thing to do is to file your application before your information finds its way into the media or another event considered a public disclosure.

The key point to remember is that allegations that a person owes taxes or committed tax fraud cannot already be found in a legal proceeding, government report, or the media if you, as an entrepreneur, want to receive a reward of between 15% and 30%.

Assume for the moment that the IRS determines that there was a public disclosure prior to the filing of your reward application and you do not meet the technical definition of an original source. The IRS Reward Program still permits, but does not require, the IRS to pay you a reward of up to 10%.

Your reward will depend on how useful your information was in the IRS investigation or the recovery of taxes. For instance, if the IRS has already opened an investigation it is not worth as much as if your application got the ball rolling. If you added nothing, the reward may be zero. But, if you found a new source of income or assets—such as a bank account or property the IRS did not already know about—that aids the IRS in recovering the taxes, a reward is more likely to be paid. Similarly, if you present new information, or if the IRS takes a different approach than anyone has taken before, then you may still receive a reward. The percentage between zero and ten all depends on how useful your information was to the IRS.

This area can be tricky for a lay person. For this reason, you may consider asking an attorney experienced with government reward programs to help you present the application to the IRS and advocate on your behalf to receive a higher reward, approaching 10%. Your attorney may also be able to argue that you meet the original source exception, which would place you into the range of 15% to 30%.

FOIA—Friend or Foe?

One final tricky area for entrepreneurs is the Freedom of Information Act (FOIA). When discussing the public disclosure bar, the question arises as to whether to use FOIA to obtain information.

If the only information you obtain is generic business data, a common reading of the IRS statute would dictate that there is no reason why the public disclosure bar should apply. However, in the DOJ Reward Program, the courts are divided over whether using

FOIA to gain information amounts to a public disclosure. It remains to be seen how the IRS will treat this issue. We already know that the IRS will ask you where you obtained the documents, so if you do use FOIA, the issue will be clearly at hand.

In addition, the government sometimes provides a copy of a FOIA request to the company that information is sought about. This occurs most commonly when the government worker trying to comply with the FOIA request has a question, and it is simple to contact the company for an answer. Thus, using FOIA may tip your hand or alert the company to your inquiry. Therefore, give careful thought to whether to make a FOIA request.

Who Cannot Apply
IRS Employees

It should be no big surprise, but IRS employees are not eligible for rewards. Of the eight specific reasons why the IRS will not even consider an application, four of them bar applications by government employees and contractors whose jobs involve reviewing federal tax returns or reporting fraud.

The initial category of restrictions upon those who cannot apply for a reward are those who:

- Are employed by the Department of Treasury (including the IRS).
- Work for any government entity and learn of tax fraud in the scope of their duties.
- Have a duty under federal law to disclose the fraud.
- Gained the information in an official capacity working for an entity with special access to government files containing federal tax returns.
- Acquired the information through access to taxpayer information, as part of a contract with the federal government which granted them access to tax returns.

Because of the special access to information these people have, you would probably expect these categories to be excluded. Indeed, laws mandate that the government not disclose tax returns to others except in the course of narrowly defined official government purposes. Using access to government files to scour tax returns for underpayments in order to line your pockets goes against protected rights of privacy. In fact, it could even be a crime for someone working for the government to gain access to tax returns for unofficial business.

The IRS statute also limits another class of applicants. As discussed in Chapter Eight, those who planned and initiated the scheme themselves may also be prohibited or receive little or no reward.

Anonymous Claims or Aliases

Another restriction is that you cannot obtain a reward by reporting it anonymously or using an alias. When submitting IRS Form 211 to apply for a reward, you must use your real name and provide your Social Security or taxpayer identification number.

However, as explained in Chapter Fourteen, the fact that you sign your name to Form 211 does not mean the IRS will disclose your name to anyone. In fact, one of the core features about this new program is that it is designed to maintain confidences. The IRS will strive hard to keep your real name from ever being made public. Of course, you are free to announce to the world when you become a millionaire.

As explained earlier, the IRS needs your real name on a signed declaration to help ensure that your information is credible and not being used to get the IRS to audit your enemy. In addition, because the reward amount is taxable income, the IRS wants to know whom they are paying so they can ensure you give them some of the money back—by claiming the reward as income.

Filing Joint Applications

There may be times where you want to join with someone else to claim a reward. The IRS permits this, provided that each person fills out and signs Form 211.

There are a few reasons favoring filing joint applications, but several why you should shy away from it. Some of the pros and cons are listed below. In the end, it is a decision you must make yourself.

> **Pros**

A joint application may be right for you if you have worked closely with someone else to ferret out the tax evasion. When you believe your friend should share equally in the fruits of your joint labor, you may wish to combine forces. You may also enjoy the camaraderie of having a partner.

Of course, if you lack sufficiently detailed information and cannot obtain it without adding another whistleblower, you may wish to join forces. But any decision to do so must be weighed against the risks discussed below.

> **Cons**

There are two phrases that top the list of arguments against adding someone to your application:

Loose lips sink ships

Nothing comes between friends like money.

If you tell a friend that you are considering filing for a reward, he may try to submit an application before you have a chance to file your own. Remember, the IRS will not disclose the names of others who file for rewards, so you may never have any idea that your friend is preparing an application—or even if they have filed an application. Until now, you may have always trusted your friend implicitly. But keep in mind that, when it comes to money, nothing has greater potential to ruin a friendship.

The general guiding principle is: Trust no one. Never tell anyone except for your attorney that you are even considering filing for a reward. You will need time to gather information and prepare a solid application without the fear that someone else may be trying to get ahead of you—because you could not keep your mouth shut.

That said, if you do need help to gain necessary information, the pros may outweigh the cons. The best advice is to first discuss this option with an attorney. He may be able to help you work with that person as a co-applicant.

Another argument against taking on co-applicants is that, whenever there are two or more people involved in an application, there are increased opportunities for squabbles. Perhaps they cannot agree upon whether to use an attorney or which attorney to use, i.e., the local attorney who does employment law or a national whistleblower attorney.

Whether or not you plan to team up with someone else, it is a good idea to let your attorney know if you have been telling other people about your plans. Again, talking about it increases the risk that someone else will file before you. So, the stakes are much higher and time is of the essence. If he is informed of this situation, your attorney may be able to speed up his process and save your first filing position for the application.

▶ Split Rewards and Tax Issues of Joint Applicants

If you plan to file jointly, you should agree in advance in writing as to the percentage each person will receive—for example, a 40–60 split or a 50–50 split. If you do not agree in advance, it will inevitably create a fight later and hard feelings. Once real dollar amounts are offered, things change. Each person's reasonable expectation is almost always different. Whatever you decide, be sure to put it in writing. Even without intent, both of you are likely to remember the agreement very differently later. If it is in writing, there will always be an indisputable reference.

Thinking through what share you plan to give up may also cause you to rethink if you need a partner. When payday arrives in a few years, you may regret giving up a large portion of the reward to someone else—especially since you will also be paying a portion to your attorney and to the IRS in income tax.

What happens when you informally agree to split a reward with someone who does not put their signature on the reward application filed with the IRS? There may be tax implications, even if you informally promise to pay a friend a portion of the reward.

Consider this example. Joe files the application himself. Three years later, the IRS pays Joe $2 million. The IRS issues a Form 1099 to Joe for the full amount of the reward. Joe however, pays his attorney one-third, or $660,000. He also pays 25% in federal and state taxes on the remaining $1.34 million, or $335,000. This leaves Joe with $1 million in his pocket.

But what if Joe promised to pay his good friend John one-half of the reward for giving him the idea in the first place? The first question is, should it be one-half net or gross? Assuming it is one-half of the net amount (after taxes and expenses), that is one-half of $1 million. So Joe pays John $500,000 and keeps $500,000 for himself.

The trouble is, John must now pay $100,000 in taxes on his $500,000. The federal and state tax boards will be happy, because they are being paid $335,000 by Joe on the initial reward and another $100,000 by John on his half. But John will not be too happy. He may even ask Joe to split the taxes with him. If Joe has to pay another $50,000, he will not be happy either.

If the friends had signed the reward application together and filed jointly, there would not be a second tax on the amount given to John. Out of the $2 million reward, both Joe and John would have received $1 million. They would have paid half of the attorney's fees ($330,000), plus half the taxes ($167,500), netting both of them $500,000.

Saving $100,000 in taxes is a good argument for filing together rather than relying upon informal commitments. Nobody likes to think of taxes while applying for a reward, but planning ahead can save you headaches later. These are exactly the kinds of considerations an attorney experienced in reward filings can warn you about before it's too late.

In summary, give thought to the net amount you will receive before deciding whether to take on a partner. And if you do, be sure to have a written agreement regarding how the money will be divided.

Conclusion

Insiders are the ideal applicants for the IRS Reward Program, since they have access to important information that will be invaluable to the IRS in prosecuting their claims and perhaps even proving intent to commit fraud. Insiders, however, are likely to collect a reward only once. Entrepreneurs are best placed to ferret out wrongdoing and collect numerous rewards, building a lucrative career. There are hurdles to cross and restrictions to consider, but a professionally prepared application, complete with specific and detailed information, will have the best odds for success.

Chapter Ten

Filing the Application: What it Takes to be Successful

*I would rather lose in a cause that will some day win,
than win in a cause that will some day lose.*

— WOODROW WILSON (1856–1924)

What does it take to bolster your chances of receiving an IRS reward? In other words: What can you do to make your application credible and convincing?

The answer to that question is as simple as one word: *documentation*. If you do not have documents to give to the IRS to support your claim, then you need an added dose of two words: *specific* and *detailed* information.

Documents—The Best Evidence

The IRS loves documents. In fact, the single most important key for the government winning or settling a tax evasion case and paying a reward is documents. Either the whistleblower must provide them or he describes them in sufficient detail so the government can subpoena them.

Why does the IRS love documents so much? A witness may lie or have faulty memory, but documents do not.

The IRS Guidance specifically addresses documents. It states that if you have documents that substantiate your claim, you must supply them to the IRS. The types of helpful documents include, but are not limited to, copies of bank statements, financial data, descriptions of assets, pertinent pages from books and records, transaction documents, emails, or memos discussing the transaction or tax issue.

Although this should not be construed as legal advice, the general guidance offered by many attorneys is that employees generally may make copies of documents they have access to in the normal course of their work. For instance, if you get an email, you may copy it. If an internal memo is sent to you, you may copy it. But you should not go rummaging through other people's offices or to places outside the scope of your normal duties to find documents and copy them. If you do not normally have access to the files you need, it is not a good idea to go looking in places that may be disallowed anyway.

There are also some limitations. First, you cannot take the original. But you can usually take a copy. Companies need their documents and taking an original may interfere with their operations. The company may even consider this theft and ask the government to file charges. Stick to making copies.

Second, you should never copy or remove documents from your employer that were prepared by company lawyers. These documents are privileged. The IRS will not even read documents written by attorneys rendering legal advice or letters from the company to the lawyer asking for advice. (Although there is a limited exception where the attorney is helping the company set up a fraudulent scheme, known as "the crime fraud exception," it is a complex issue that a lay person should not try to assess.)

Third, you should refrain from taking documents that contain true trade secrets. If the document contains proprietary information, don't take it. Chances are that it won't really help you explain why taxes were underpaid and, again, it can be considered theft.

Fourth, with respect to emails, be very careful not to violate the electronic policies set by the company. For instance, some companies do not allow you to forward or send emails to computers outside the office or to third parties, which may include an email account to which another person has access. Therefore, you may wish to print the emails or copy them to a disk or thumb drive, if you cannot print them at work.

The documents you gather do not need to detail the whole fraud scheme. But they should provide support to your allegation that the taxpayer has, in fact, underpaid taxes. In addition, make copies only of documents worth the risk. Do not make copies just to fill a folder or box. Quantity does not necessarily equal quality. A single smoking gun document can be worth more than a room full of general documents.

Even if you do not have copies of the documents themselves, the IRS will want information about documents that you know exist. For instance, you may not have direct access to the books, but you can describe for the IRS the way the accounting books are kept and where they are located. Describing all the relevant documents you know of and their potential locations will help the IRS prove its case. The IRS also welcomes the names and locations of bank accounts. Basically, give it all the information it may rely upon to prove that the person has underpaid taxes. It is also a good idea to draw a picture of the offices or areas where documents exist to help describe where they are located, in case the IRS wants to issue a subpoena or use a search warrant.

But, let's make this perfectly clear: Do not take unnecessary risks in trying to get copies of documents. First, you risk alerting the person that you suspect them of fraud and risk getting caught. If you get caught, you may get fired. Even if you get documents, there is no guarantee that the IRS will pay a reward, and even if it does, it may be 5 or 6 years later.

On a related note, there are some risks in secretly recording telephone calls to support your claim. Although many states allow a person to secretly record a telephone call they are on, in many other states it is illegal without the consent of all parties to a call. You definitely want to know the rules in your state before taping calls.

If you have personal knowledge, but cannot obtain documents in support, the strength of your knowledge will be the key. At a minimum, you must be able to articulate just how the tax evasion is being committed. In order to convince a busy IRS agent to open an investigation, you must base your evidence upon very detailed and specific facts. The next section addresses the information you should provide in your application.

Attach a Clear, Concise, and Complete Memo

To receive a reward, you must do more than simply meet the dollar threshold amounts and submit the IRS Form 211. You must provide the IRS with a detailed submission describing the tax evasion, the evidence in support, the amount of underpayments, and the legal and factual reasons why taxes are owed.

When examining IRS Form 211 (see Appendix D), you should notice that lines 15 and 16 call for narratives, which, if done properly, could not possibly fit in the small spaces provided on the form. In fact, those line items indicate that you may use continuation sheets. Actually, attaching a carefully crafted statement of material evidence in support of the allegations is more of a requirement than a suggestion.

As indicated above, the IRS expects you to provide photocopies of relevant documents in your possession. Of course, your submission must describe them and why they are important. If you do not have documents, the memo you attach is all the more critical.

When you or your attorney prepare the memo attached to the application, begin by outlining the tax evasion allegations. In a logical and orderly manner, walk the reader through each step. Describe the tax issue, whether it is a deduction that is not allowable or income not being claimed. For each element or issue, explain why it amounts to underpaid taxes and what evidence you have to prove it.

This means you include names of people and dates of events. You describe how and why actions were taken and why they were improper. If you have documents to prove a point, identify the documents and how and why they support your claim. Attach such documents as a numbered tab to the memo.

Be sure to include a discussion of how much in taxes went underpaid and how you calculated this amount.

Do not neglect discussing your knowledge. Be upfront about whether you were asked to participate or help conceal the tax evasion. Tell the IRS when and how you learned of the information. Describe your relationship (past or present) to the person or company you allege underpaid taxes. For instance, tell the IRS whether you are a family member, employee, partner, accountant, customer, or acquaintance.

You should be getting the message that the IRS wants much more than a one-page form or short explanation. Pretend that the IRS asked you to provide a detailed memo outlining the allegations, the evidence or proof, the manner in which damages were calculated, the documentary support for the allegations, and the relationship you have to the person or company. Do not wait to be asked this information. Expect that the IRS needs it to open an investigation.

In sum, although not a technical requirement, the IRS is asking you to attach a lengthy memorandum to Form 211. It is similar to the type of memorandum lawyers provide to a judge when arguing a legal position. If you do not provide detailed information, it may affect whether a reward is ultimately paid.

Preparing the Memo

The approach used by seasoned whistleblower attorneys is to type into Boxes 14 to 16 on Form 211 the phrase: "See attached memorandum." In other words, you or your attorney need to prepare a statement of material evidence in support of your allegations. As indicated earlier, this memo functions as a roadmap of your allegations. It ensures that the IRS does not misunderstand your allegations; at the same time it tells a story of tax evasion which spurs the IRS agent to open a case.

There is an art to writing persuasively that simultaneously incorporates the "three C's of persuasive writing":

- Clear
- Concise
- Complete

Your memo needs to be clear, so that the IRS does not misunderstand your allegations or jump to a wrong conclusion. That can be fatal. You may never know that they did not understand your allegations or get a second chance. The memo should have a logical structure, including an introduction that sets the tone.

The memo also needs to be concise, yet complete. Certainly, you must include all of the information necessary to support your allegations completely. But the information must also be concise, crisp and clean. If you drone on and repeat yourself, the reader will get bored and put down your packet. You definitely need to keep their attention and want them to keep turning pages rather than move to a different application. Strive for a fine balance between being concise and complete.

Do not grudgingly approach preparing the statement of material evidence. This is your chance to stand out. It is where you set the tone for the case. It is one of the few things you can control in this process. Don't wait until the IRS calls and asks for an interview; give it the best you have upfront in this memorandum.

Contents of the Memo

What should go in the memo? A detailed description of the allegations is the beginning point for drafting a statement of material evidence. The description indicates why you contend the taxpayer underpaid taxes, and if they cheated, why the tax return was fraudulent.

In addition to outlining in a methodical manner the nature, extent, and proof of the unpaid taxes, you should tie into the discussion the relevance of documents in support. You also need to provide the names of key fact witnesses that can support your allegations and discuss the knowledge of each person.

Any documents you have should be labeled and attached. There is nothing better than giving the government a smoking gun document, such as an email or internal company memo outlining or admitting tax fraud. Even documents that simply help understand the transaction or events are welcomed by the IRS and must be described and attached.

In a conversational style, you or your attorney must tell the IRS the real scoop about the case. The memo needs to explain things such that the assigned IRS agent will want to invest time, resources, and energy into your case. Therefore, highlight the strengths of the case, including any and all admissions by the defendants.

Using simple words and structure, you need to show why this is a solid case of underpayment of taxes, or even fraud, and what evidence you have to prove it. Do not try to sound like an accountant or lawyer. And certainly do not oversell your case. Maintain your credibility.

You or your attorney should also discuss damages without overselling your case, as well. Be sure to differentiate between amount of unreported income and amount of unpaid taxes.

Writing a memo that accomplishes these goals is a lot of work. It is also difficult to write clearly, concisely, and completely all at the same time. But it is extremely important. In fact, preparing this memo will likely reveal some weak points in your case. You may discover that you need to gather more information to position yourself to tell a great story. It is worth the effort to do this right because the IRS will be pleased to write the conclusion if you present a great plot.

Staying on Task and Avoiding Fluff

As you begin preparing your application and memo in support, you need to give thought to what allegations to include or exclude. For instance, if your main allegation is that a person formed an improper trust and did not include the income on their taxes, do you want to also allege that they claimed one too many child deductions? Sometimes people think it strengthens core allegations to include every other possible wrong that may conceivably have been committed. This is a shotgun approach, where you blast everything in the hopes that something will find its mark.

There are problems with a shotgun approach. First, the reader may think you are guessing or that you simply have an axe to grind. They may also shake their head, thinking to themselves, "This will take a lifetime to try to sort out." What you think may strengthen the case may actually weaken it.

In addition, your credibility is on the line. Just as a chain is measured by the strength of the weakest link, your allegations may also be viewed that way. For instance, if an experienced IRS agent reads one of your allegations and knows that it is not tax evasion, based upon his own experience, he may consider your whole application suspect.

It is best to go with your strongest allegation first and consider reducing, or even eliminating weak allegations. The worst thing you can do is lose credibility with the government or have them view your application as an Easter egg hunt.

You can include some additional allegations along with your main one, but there is an art to preparing a memorandum that garners interest and establishes credibility—while also including allegations that may lack sufficient support now, but are likely to yield fruit during the investigation of the solid claim. Once the government is convinced about your lead allegation, they may become more willing to devote time to investigate your less well-developed allegations.

The bottom line is that you need to give it careful thought before including any allegation for which you do not have full support. If you decide it adds value, even though it is less supported, then make sure your memo treats that claim differently so the reader knows you recognize that it is a more speculative possibility—unlike your lead allegation. Also, leave it for last, after you win over the busy IRS agent with a clear, concise, complete, and convincing memorandum fully detailing and supporting your lead allegation.

Pursuing Older Claims

One additional point needs to be made regarding the preparation of a successful application. In situations where your claims are older or outside the standard statute of limitation, the need for documents is even greater. As explained in Chapter Eight, the tradeoff for having no statute of limitation for fraud cases requires that you prove fraudulent intent by clear and convincing evidence. That is a very high standard. In addition, older cases have additional hurdles, such as fading memories or missing files.

To convince the IRS to take an older case, there really should be a smoking gun. Your description of the fraud scheme and evidence of intent needs to be not only clearly described, but backed up with credible and detailed factual evidence. Again, documents are the key, unless you have what amounts to a confession that you or someone else is willing to testify to in court, if needed.

If you can prove tax fraud, great! It is worth the effort because without a statute of limitation, you can receive double or triple the amount of a standard three-year allegation of unpaid taxes. Just be prepared to work even harder at outlining your case using the techniques discussed earlier.

Conclusion

The IRS is not interested in hunches or speculation. For instance, if your neighbor owns five cars but works as a cashier at a fast food store, don't expect the IRS to open a file. In addition, if a store fails to give you a receipt when you paid cash, that is not sufficient to prove they make a habit of failing to report store income. It is not enough to know in your heart that a person must be cheating on their tax returns. You need specifics.

As may be expected, the IRS receives numerous reports of "suspected cheating." It also frequently encounters suspicions gone wild. The IRS lacks resources to investigate vague allegations.

An IRS reward is reserved for those who can specifically show how a taxpayer owes taxes. It is done by providing concrete proof. The most common method is by producing records that "document" the unpaid taxes or tax fraud. Perhaps you know of a second set of books and you copied several pages. You may have other types of documents, such as a collection of internal memos, letters, or emails.

You can still win the IRS over to your case without documents. The key to any successful application is to take the time to carefully prepare a memorandum in support of your application. Remember, the IRS is looking for detailed and specific evidence of unpaid taxes.

Chapter Eleven

Should You Use an Attorney?

No person was ever honored for what he received.
Honor has been the reward for what he gave.

— Calvin Coolidge (1872–1933)

Whether or not to use an attorney can be a very difficult decision. Unlike the DOJ Reward Program where you must use an attorney to file your claim because it requires filing a formal action in court, the IRS Reward Program does not require the help of legal counsel.

Under the old IRS Informant program, the help of attorneys was discouraged, if not forbidden. Partly as a result of excluding the use of legal representation, the IRS was able to act arbitrarily in deciding who to give rewards to and what percentage to pay. As discussed in Chapter Three, the amount of rewards to these unrepresented citizens was often less than 2%, and citizens had no way of knowing if the IRS had simply used their information without paying their reward.

Today, however, the new IRS Reward Program allows, and even encourages, the use of attorneys. This raises a new question about whether and when it is in the best interest of a person to file an application alone or hire an attorney.

Weighing whether the added value is worth the cost is not unique to attorney fees. Congress and the IRS faced a similar issue when establishing the new whistleblower program. A decision had to be made whether it was worth it to pay whistleblowers up to 30% of taxes collected. For the IRS, the cost-benefit analysis favored paying rewards, even though it meant giving up a share of the recovery. You face a similar decision.

If you believe there is value added by an attorney, then it makes economic sense for you to share the reward with an attorney. Of course, you may decide that what an attorney brings to the table is not worth giving up one-third of the reward. Because the IRS Reward Program does not require you to use an attorney, it is a decision you need to make. Below is a discussion of some of the factors you may wish to consider.

Reasons Why You Should Use an Attorney

One particular value added by hiring an attorney experienced with government reward programs is that he is more likely to prepare an application that appeals to a busy IRS agent trying to decide which cases warrant opening an investigation. In addition, if your attorney has significant experience with government reward programs, an IRS agent may be more willing to open an investigation in your particular case. Your attorney's reputation may lend credibility to your application.

A seasoned whistleblower attorney will do a good job of explaining the allegations and why and how much there is in unpaid taxes. He will also be able to suggest to the IRS agent an investigative strategy that appears well-reasoned and sound. In short, you are hiring an attorney to present the case in a manner that entices.

Remember, there is no appeal process if the IRS declines to open an investigation. You cannot force the IRS to investigate your allegations. They can pick from those on their desks and decide which sound most promising.

Perhaps the agent may wonder whether the *pro se* applicant was unable to find an attorney willing to take the case. In other words, if many people use attorneys to aid them with large dollar cases, but you do not, will the agent wonder whether it was because no attorney would take your case?

You may not know this, but attorneys carefully screen cases before agreeing to represent whistleblowers. They turn down far more whistleblower reward cases than they take. For every 20 cases presented to an experienced whistleblower counsel, only one will be accepted. Most are turned down because they do not meet the technical requirements. The rest of the rejected cases are where the allegations are either too vague or lack the detail and specificity the IRS expects. (Hopefully, this book will change these statistics so that applicants not meeting the requirements will not pursue cases and those who can meet the requirements will prepare more thorough applications.)

The IRS is not ignorant of the screening process used by attorneys in these matters. In fact, they welcome it. They appreciate it when attorneys weed out cases that do not meet the technical requirements or are too weak to warrant filing. This saves the IRS time and resources. In fact, the IRS Whistleblower Office regularly attends annual meetings held by whistleblower counsel and provides them with updates and other information regarding the program. They also openly discuss what the IRS looks for in successful applications. In short, the IRS considers legal counsel a part of the team.

Beyond perceptions by the IRS, an experienced attorney can also add value by being an advocate for the whistleblower. Perhaps the IRS agent will be more willing to talk to an attorney than a *pro se* applicant. You may have experienced this before, when a company does not return your call but they respond when an attorney calls. Thus, an attorney may get more opportunities to talk to the IRS than you may on your own. The attorney may even convince an agent to kick the tires again before declining or gain a second opportunity to explain how and why this case is worth the time.

In addition, once back taxes are collected by the IRS, you want to make sure you receive a fair reward. Simply having an attorney works to your benefit at this final stage. The Whistleblower Office knows that if it awards you less than the maximum amount, the whistleblower may file an appeal with the federal Tax Court in Washington, D.C. Just knowing that you have hired legal counsel may make the IRS more inclined to give a higher reward in order to avoid an appeal, which may require them to pay you the maximum amount *in addition to* legal fees.

An attorney can also be a great asset if there is an issue regarding public disclosure, which can reduce the reward to the 0% to 10% category. Will a *pro se* whistleblower know how to argue that his allegations were not principally based upon public information or how to effectively argue that the original source exception applies? Will an applicant's attorney know how to argue his allegations?

The strength of your attorney in convincing the IRS can really make a difference. For instance, an informed attorney can submit a legal memorandum citing cases to convince the Whistleblower Office that the public disclosure bar does not apply or that you meet the original source exception.

If these issues arise, you will wish you had counsel that is familiar with these standards. The good news is that, unlike the DOJ program, the defendant is not allowed to argue that you do not deserve a reward or meet the requirements. This gives you a distinct advantage. In DOJ cases, the party you have made allegations against can enlist a high-priced attorney to argue that you are not eligible for a reward. In IRS cases, that cannot happen. Your reward is negotiated solely between your attorney and the IRS.

In addition, the reward program is built upon ranges of rewards. That means you can negotiate a percentage. Will you be as effective as an attorney in this area? Perhaps, but it is possible that the IRS will not even attempt to negotiate an amount with you, as a *pro se* applicant, but will instead send a letter in the mail with the amount it determines.

Finally, because the appeal rights available under the IRS Reward Program are expressly limited to filing a legal proceeding before the Tax Court, this step will require you to hire an attorney, even if you haven't been using one from the start. A lay person simply won't be expected to handle an appeal to a federal court in Washington, D.C. on a *pro se* basis. Besides, what sense would it make to hire an attorney only after the IRS decides to reduce your reward, rather than prevent that reduction in the first place?

One Reason Not to Use an Attorney

The biggest reason not to use an attorney is that he will charge you a contingency fee for representing you.

Because IRS whistleblower cases often take years to complete and there is no guarantee of a reward, the most common way to hire an attorney is to agree to give them a percentage of the reward. This is known as a contingency fee.

To hire a quality attorney experienced with government whistle-blower reward programs, expect to pay a contingency fee rate of 40%, although some firms charge 33.33% and others as high as 50%. The only payment they receive is a portion of your reward. The fee is for their service in filing the reward application, communicating and negotiating with the IRS, and possibly appealing a low reward amount to the Tax Court.

While the rate certainly affects the ultimate amount you will receive, you should not select your attorney based upon the lowest rates. Any attorney can hold himself out as qualified in virtually any area of the law, whether it is personal injury, antitrust law, or whistleblower protection work. Since it is important for you to find an attorney experienced in winning rewards for his clients, you will want to inquire into his background and experience.

Do not make the mistaken assumption that the firm with the highest rate is better than one charging an average rate. Most people tend to associate cost with value, but this assumption is not always justified.

Don't begrudge your attorney his fees. By taking your case without being paid up front, your attorney is giving up the opportunity to work on other matters at his normal billing rate. In addition, included in these costs are amounts of out-of-pocket expenses that the client would bear without an attorney.

What to Expect From Your Attorney

As you weigh the decision whether to file for a reward, consider all that will be required from your attorney to prepare a proper filing and follow the case to conclusion. Below are examples of the legal work to expect from your attorney during each stage of the IRS Reward Program.

As you can imagine, each of these tasks requires significant whistleblower reward experience and skill. It will also require some effort by you, as well as staying power. You and your attorney will be earning your IRS reward. Below are the roles of your attorney.

Pre-Filing Stage
- Listening carefully to your story
- Creating an investigative plan
- Analyzing whether you can meet all of the requirements
- Helping you weigh personal risks against potential rewards
- Conducting legal research regarding tax issues
- Conducting legal research regarding reward requirements
- Gathering background information about the cheating taxpayer
- Researching assets and ability to pay issues
- Contacting the IRS, as needed
- Evaluating who underpaid taxes
- Calculating the underpayment of taxes
- Creating a customized and convincing statement of material evidence
- Filing the submission

Post-Filing Stage
- Preparing you, as the whistleblower, for an IRS interview
- Obtaining additional information if requested by the IRS
- Explaining the allegations to the IRS to ensure they understand them
- Responding to questions or requests from the IRS
- Conducting additional research, as needed
- Creating damage models and calculations
- Maintaining regular contact with the IRS
- Keeping the client informed of progress or new events

Settlement—Setting the Amount of Reward
- Negotiating a fair reward amount with the IRS
- Arguing why you belong in the 15% to 30% range (not the 0% to 10% range)
- Presenting valid reasons supporting increases in the rate beyond the minimum
- Appealing the reward amount to the Tax Court if it is too low

Cases Under $5 Million

Cases that have the best chance of success without legal counsel are those under $5 million in unpaid taxes. First, it is difficult to attract the more experienced whistleblower attorneys with cases under $5 million. Second, if you cannot locate an attorney who has extensive experience with government reward programs, you may not get the value added advice needed to tip the balance in favor of using counsel.

If you are to proceed solo, you must be able to honestly appraise your own abilities. Can you prepare a clear, concise, and complete description of the allegations, including why the taxes are owed, how much has been unpaid, and how many documents you have to support the allegations? If you can do this and confidently explain these things to the IRS in an interview, you may be qualified to file your own smaller-dollar case.

Claiming a Reward for Reporting Tax Evasion—Without Using an Attorney

If you elect to file for a reward without the help of counsel, be sure to carefully follow all of the requirements. In addition to reading this book, visit the IRS website at *www.IRS.gov*. Toward the top of the page you should see a white box where you can type a search term and then click on the search button. If you type in the term "whistleblower reward," then click search, the website will list links to the reward program.

As you read through the description of the program, there will be a link to Form 211. You can fill it out online and then print it. Of course, you should also submit a memo in support following the suggestions in this book.

Forgoing the Reward

Not everyone wants to go through the effort of submitting an application for a reward, but some may want to alert the IRS to tax evasion for its own sake. If you decide that you don't want to claim a reward, but still want to report the tax fraud to the IRS, Chapter Fourteen contains information on how to do that.

Conclusion

In the end, whether to hire an attorney and which attorney to hire are subjective decisions each person must make for himself. But this should be carefully thought through up front. Cases under $5 million are the best candidates for going solo—but only if you know your own limits. You must be able to effectively prepare an enticing application that also meets all of the technical requirements. Keeping 100% of the reward only matters if a reward is paid.

Chapter Twelve
The IRS Investigation

If men were angels, no government would be necessary.
— James Madison (1751–1836)

There is a shroud of mystery surrounding how the IRS works, even with respect to its whistleblower reward program. The IRS Guidance sheds very little light on the situation. In fact, it states that the IRS will not tell you about their investigations or provide you with any status reports or updates on reward applications.

What little they tell you can be summarized in two sentences: The IRS makes no commitments about whether you will receive a reward or how long the process will take, but the entire process could take years. Because the reward can only be paid out of proceeds collected from the taxpayer, it can take at least three to six years to receive a reward.

What to Expect During the Investigative Period

What about the role of the IRS and what does the process look like? The IRS has not provided any formal guidance on this. However, fairly accurate predictions can be made from experience with the related DOJ Reward Program and applications that have actually been submitted under the new IRS Reward Program. The next section walks you through the process and gives you a pretty good idea of what to expect.

Acknowledgement of Receipt

After the reward application is submitted, it is assigned to an analyst who works for the Whistleblower Office. The analysts are located in different parts of the country such as Ft. Lauderdale, Florida, Buffalo, New York, or Houston, Texas.

The assigned analyst reviews the application to ensure that all of the technical requirements have been met, such as the use of Form 211, the signature of the applicant, the amount of alleged unpaid taxes is $2 million (including penalties), and that all other required forms and information have been provided.

Only one analyst is assigned to each application, and that person will be the primary point of contact with the whistleblower or his attorney. You will contact the analyst with any questions or to supply any additional information.

Once the analyst is satisfied that the application appears in order, he does two things. First, he sends a letter to the whistleblower. (A sample letter with text from a real case can be found in Appendix F.) The letter informs the person that the application was received and a claim number was assigned. The letter provides the following guidance to the whistleblower:

> The information you provided will be evaluated to determine if an investigation is warranted and an award is appropriate. Although we may need to contact you to discuss the information submitted, we cannot tell you specific details about what actions we will be taking, if any, using the information you gave us. Internal Revenue Code Section 6103 protects the tax information of all taxpayers and prevents us from making these disclosures. At the conclusion of the review and investigation, we will only be able to tell you whether or not the information you provided met our criteria for paying an award.[11]

Second, the letter provides the whistleblower with the name of the Whistleblower Office analyst and his telephone number.

IRS Appoints a Subject Matter Expert

The Whistleblower Office analyst forwards the application and all other information provided by the whistleblower to a "subject matter expert." This is a person or team of individuals within the IRS that receive training or possess specialized knowledge most similar to the allegations being made by the whistleblower.

The subject matter expert reviews the information to determine the nature of the allegations and decides which investigative IRS agent the matter should be assigned to, if at all. As discussed below, if the subject matter expert does not believe that the allegations are specific and credible on their face, he can close the file. In that event, you will receive a rejection letter a few months later which cannot be appealed.

IRS Creates a Taint Team

The subject matter expert will also analyze whether any of the information provided by the applicant is "tainted." Thus, the subject matter expert or team of experts is also known as the "clean team" or "taint team." For instance, if the whistleblower attached copies of documents written by the taxpayer's attorney or are otherwise privileged or inadmissible evidence, they will remove that information before sending the information to an assigned IRS agent responsible for investigating the allegations. (It is the assigned IRS investigative agent, not the subject matter expert, who decides what ultimate action, if any, the IRS should take against the taxpayer, including recovery of unpaid taxes.) As part of this same process, the subject matter expert, or clean team, will interview or debrief the whistleblower.

The case analyst will coordinate the meeting by sending the whistleblower or their attorney a letter to schedule a meeting. However, the case analyst will not participate in the interview by the clean team.

The purpose of the debriefing is to clarify the submission, gain any additional information relevant to the claim, assess whether any of the information is privileged, assess any evidentiary issues that may arise (i.e., will the evidence be admissible in court, if needed?), and explore the relationship between the whistleblower and the taxpayer.

The goal is for the clean team to be able to pass along credible, relevant information to the assigned IRS agents and auditors. After the meeting, they will remove or redact information that is potentially privileged or may otherwise compromise the IRS investigation, then provide your clean file to the agents assigned to investigate the case.

Of course, not every person who submits an application will get an interview. If it appears on its face that your claim does not meet the requirements or have sufficient detail to warrant opening a case, you can expect to simply receive a rejection letter.

The Interview will be Tape Recorded

Don't be caught off guard. Your interview with the IRS will be tape recorded. Taping may be needed under the IRS Reward Program because the person conducting the interview will not be the same IRS agent investigating the allegations. Thus, they need to be able to pass on to the investigators the transcript of the tape rather than just notes of the meeting.

If you are willing to travel to the location of the interview, the interview may be in person, or it may be by telephone. It is also likely that several IRS employees will be participating. The meeting will typically last two or three hours.

Just because you get an interview does not mean that a case will be opened. It simply means that you passed the first screening test. The interview is your first, and perhaps only, time to win the IRS over. As explained below, the results of your interview will determine the next step: whether the case is closed or an investigation opened.

Your Attorney is not a Potted Plant during the Interview

Your attorney does not need to be a potted plant during the interview. In other words, he does not need to simply sit next to his client to show moral support. Rather, he has a role, which includes clarifying questions asked by the IRS and answers by his client. The attorney can also interject and identify information relevant to the claim which the whistleblower may have forgotten to mention.

During one IRS interview, the IRS began probing issues relevant to the public disclosure bar, but the client lacked clarity on what the IRS was asking and what issue was being probed. The attorney stepped in and informed the IRS that in addition to factual information being discussed by his client, there were also legal considerations that demonstrated his original source status. He referred the IRS agents to the portion of the submission which addressed the public disclosure bar and why his client met the original source exception.

During the interview, the attorney also made additional comments and provided information regarding the allegations to ensure that the IRS fully understood the extent of the allegations and establishing that the client met the technical requirements to receive a reward. This type of intervention is but one example of how an attorney can be invaluable in protecting your interests with the IRS.

Questions about the Allegations

Because the IRS agent conducting the interview and reviewing the materials for taint will make a recommendation as to whether a formal investigation should be opened, it is very important for the whistleblower to be fully prepared for this meeting and to present all relevant information to the IRS.

At the initial meeting, the whistleblower and his attorney will explain the allegations to the subject matter expert. Typically, the IRS will ask questions directed to the whistleblower. They are judging the whistleblower's credibility, so they will want to hear the allegations first-hand from the whistleblower. Nevertheless, the whistleblower's attorney is permitted to interject comments, as needed. In fact, they need to actively participate to ensure that the IRS understands the allegations.

In advance of the interview, the IRS agents will have read the entire submission and reviewed all the documents provided by the whistleblower. Expect that they will be very knowledgeable about the allegations and ask specific questions, beyond simply asking you to describe why you think the taxpayer underpaid taxes or committed fraud. For instance, if you allege that a company did not report a certain income stream, expect the clean team to ask you all of the what, when, how, and why questions. They may also ask how you know that they did not report the income. In short, they want to know everything about your allegations that will be helpful to them in proving that taxes were underpaid.

Be aware that you will be asked if you are willing to testify in court, if that is needed for the case. You can say no, and still receive a reward. As explained in Chapter Fourteen, the IRS asks this question in the event the only way they can prove tax evasion is with your testimony. By saying yes, you can highlight your willingness to face risks when asking for a higher percentage of a reward.

In addition, also expect to be asked to identify any other potential witnesses or documents.

Questions about Documents

Assuming you have provided documents, the IRS will ask when and how you gathered them. They will want to make sure that you did not violate any privileges, such as giving the IRS a memorandum from the taxpayer's attorney. The IRS agents may also ask the whistleblower a few substantive questions about the meaning of some documents, if clarification is needed.

Recommendations by the IRS Agents

After interviewing the whistleblower, the assigned subject matter expert from the clean team will either recommend that the IRS open a formal investigation into the allegations or close the case without further action.

If the IRS subject matter expert determines that the allegations do not appear credible or warrant opening an investigation, they will ask the assigned IRS case analyst to send the whistleblower a rejection letter. Once the rejection letter is sent, the case is closed. That is the end of the road. The program does not permit the whistleblower to second-guess or appeal a decision not to open an investigation.

The Next Steps

If the subject matter experts determine that the allegations warrant further investigation, they will forward the whistleblower's application and all information gained during the debriefing with the whistleblower (minus any privileged documents), including information provided by your attorney, to an investigative IRS agent experienced with this type of allegation.

In short, a case file is now formally opened and an IRS agent is assigned to investigate the allegations. Each IRS agent receives hundreds of new cases each year, and they must prioritize them. An auditor may also be assigned to assist the investigator.

Swirling through the mind of the assigned IRS agent and auditor receiving the case file after it clears the taint team are thoughts like these:

- How much evidence did the whistleblower provide?
- Is it enough to warrant a full-blown investigation?
- What additional information will I need to prove that the taxpayer underpaid or cheated on their taxes?
- Are damages provable by existing records of the defendant? Can I obtain them?

The investigative agent or auditor will conduct whatever investigation or audit they deem appropriate. Again, the whistleblower has no right or ability to require the IRS to take any action or to ask the IRS to recover any unpaid taxes. The IRS has unreviewable discretion to close the case or settle for any amount they determine appropriate in light of all circumstances. That is why submitting a clear, concise, and complete memorandum is so important and why your interview matters so much. If you do not entice the agents with specific and detailed information, they may not find it worth the effort compared to other cases assigned to them.

Providing Additional Information

If the whistleblower learns new information and wants to provide it to the IRS agent, he must provide it to the assigned whistleblower analyst, who will forward it to the taint team. The taint team leader may request that you copy him on communications so that he knows there are additions to the file. (You can also volunteer to provide a copy of any attachments to him.)

Wait Patiently

The IRS regulations do not permit the IRS to disclose information to the whistleblower regarding the status of the investigation.

Because it can take up to six years for the action to be resolved, the whistleblower must wait patiently.

Again, the whistleblower will not be able to challenge, contest, or appeal whether the IRS agent opens a case file or how much money, if any, the IRS agent recovers. As discussed below, the only appeal opportunity is to contest the percentage of an actual reward before the Tax Court.

If the IRS recovers funds from the taxpayer, then the Whistleblower Office will determine the amount of a reward, if any. Specifically, the Director of the Whistleblower Office in Washington, D.C., with input from his local staff, will determine the amount. In arriving at the amount, his office will coordinate with the case analyst. That office will also receive input and recommendations from the IRS agent and auditors when determining the eligibility of the whistleblower for a reward and the exact amount.

After this consultation, the IRS case analyst will notify the whistleblower of the decision regarding the amount of any reward to be paid. Do not, however, expect the IRS to provide details regarding how the decision was reached. Rather, the whistleblower will receive a letter stating how much the reward is and what percentage of the amount the IRS recovered. It will contain information about the right to an appeal and perhaps a few publicly available details, but it won't list the reasons or analysis of how the reward amount was reached.

The whistleblower's attorney can contact the Whistleblower's Office to discuss the matter, but do not expect your attorney to receive a lot of details either. More than likely, he will receive just enough information to formulate a decision on whether to appeal the reward amount.

If you disagree with the IRS as to the amount of the reward or a determination that you are not entitled to a portion of the amount the IRS recovered, your attorney may appeal that decision to the U.S. Tax Court. Because the program is so new, there have not yet been any Tax Court decisions.

One Way Flow of Information

The IRS Guidance does not outright tell you that the flow of information is one way only, but that is the case. When speaking to

IRS agents, they will remind you again and again that they are pro-hibited from sharing information with you. The IRS will not discuss with you any information regarding the status of the investigation. It will not even tell you whether another person has previously filed for a reward on the same matter.

It is even possible that you could wait one or more years before hearing a word from the IRS. Then, suddenly you receive a letter from your IRS case analyst stating that you can expect a reward of $1 million and that you were awarded 21%!

At that point, you will receive only the basic facts about the status of the case, such as how much the IRS actually recovered from the taxpayer. You will know just enough information for your attorney to make a determination whether to appeal the amount of the reward to the Tax Court.

Prior chapters discuss your role in negotiating the reward and how exact percentages are fixed. The next chapter discusses your options if the IRS declines your submission.

Conclusion

Although there remains some mystery to the IRS investigative process, the IRS will conduct its investigation in a manner similar to other agencies, including the Department of Justice, when analyzing whistleblower claims. The key to this program is that the flow of information is even more one-directional, which makes your initial submission and resulting interview all the more critical.

Chapter Thirteen
Why the IRS Rejects Cases

Not long ago, a man in Oklahoma, named Jerome, opened his mailbox to find a letter from the IRS—a letter he was waiting to receive. His eyes lit up and his heart raced with anticipation. He had been anxious to find out if he received a reward for reporting tax evasion, but had not heard anything for a long time. When he saw the envelope, all of Jerome's dreams about buying his dream home on a lake with the reward money came flooding back to him. He was almost scared to open the envelope.

Inside, the letterhead was from the Whistleblower Office. Jerome scanned quickly to find a $ sign, hoping for many zeros behind it. His joy suddenly turned to disappointment. This was nothing but a form letter notifying him that his application had not contained enough specific and credible information to warrant an investigation. That was it. His application was rejected. Jerome did not get a reward. And he had no other recourse.

Obviously, Jerome thought he had provided the IRS with enough information. He was careful in preparing his application, but without knowing why the IRS rejects applications, he hadn't really known what to expect.

Knowing why the IRS rejects cases is valuable for two reasons. First, you can spare yourself time and energy by choosing not to file the kind of case that is unlikely to receive a reward. Second, you may be able to prepare your application in a manner that sets it apart from the types of cases the IRS frowns upon.

As you are discovering by reading this book, there are numerous, concrete things you can do to make your application more appealing, assuming your allegations meet the minimum requirements. It is important to pay close attention to each of these things, since they can dramatically improve your chances of getting a reward.

But, what if your application is rejected? This chapter discusses your options should you receive the dreaded rejection letter.

Tight Lips

The Whistleblower Office will not give you many specifics about why it rejected your case. The rejection letter will likely either state that your claim failed to meet the program requirements or the IRS found that your claim lacked specific and credible information.

As indicated earlier, the IRS has commented that 90% of information it receives lacks enough details for the IRS to even open an investigation. This book seeks to change all of that. It is essential to not only meet the technical requirements and dollar thresholds, but to also put your best foot forward in the application process. *You can avoid the most common mistakes.*

Bad Odds for Bad Cases

If you talk to seasoned attorneys who specialize in representing whistleblowers who file for rewards under government reward programs, you will find they have one thing in common. They all turn away far more cases than they take. Most law firms practicing in this area turn down 19 out of 20 applicants seeking representation in filing for a reward.

The single most common reason for declining cases is that the application lacks specific and credible information. Remarkably enough, many people step forward with nothing more than suspicions. They cannot identify a specific improper tax deduction or failure to report taxable income.

The second most common reason that attorneys turn away cases is that the allegations do not meet the minimum technical requirements. Even though the guidelines are clear, it is surprising how many people will ask an attorney to help them file a reward application when the amount of unpaid taxes is less than $2 million or where the allegations involve an individual taxpayer who does not earn $200,000 in gross income in a single relevant year.

Although it is still possible to receive a reward under the IRS's old Informant Reward Program for cases under $2 million in unpaid taxes, the rewards are so highly discretionary and the maximum percentage is so low, that few, if any, attorneys consider it worth their time.

Reasons the IRS Turns Down Cases

Regardless of whether an attorney likes your case, the real question is whether the IRS will like it. There are four main reasons the IRS rejects cases:

1. Lack of resources to open an investigation.
2. Amount of unpaid taxes, if any, is not evident from the application.
3. Facts are too speculative.
4. Motives are suspicious.

1. Lack of Resources

Remember, there are thousands of allegations of tax evasion each year. The IRS is not able to assign investigators for every allegation. In addition to formal reward applications, the IRS must also wade through allegations made on its hotline and other anonymous reports.

It may help you understand the process if you imagine the process as being similar to that of triage on a battlefield. Each allegation gets a cursory first look and a snap judgment as to whether it should be a priority. Once the decision is made, that's the end of it. A doctor on a battlefield is too busy to second-guess his decisions. The same is true at the IRS. Only if time permits does a busy IRS agent go back to reconsider allegations that did not stand out. It is unlikely that time will present itself, because new allegations keep pouring in.

Certain judgments must be made upon the potential merits of a case. That begins with how specific the allegations are regarding the scope of the tax evasion and how well they are presented to the IRS in the memo attached to Form 211. In short, absent specific and credible information, the IRS will not open an investigation.

Don't misunderstand. The IRS takes tax evasion allegations seriously. Every case gets a fair shake, but obviously some deserve and receive more attention than others. Be glad you now know how the system works and what you can do to increase your chances: hire quality counsel and present your application in a manner that demonstrates it is worthy of the time and resources necessary to win a big tax evasion case. The key is to prepare an application that stands out.

2. Amount of Unpaid Taxes

Another common problem with most allegations in reward applications is that they fail to contain enough specific details demonstrating that the minimum threshold dollar amounts are met. Most applications simply state that the losses are "in the millions" or are "substantial." Very little effort or time, however, is spent on discussing precisely *how* the taxpayer underpaid over $2 million in taxes or how it can be quantified.

In addition, many applications fail to meet one or more of the procedural and substantive requirements of the statute. If the application does not set forth allegations that establish threshold eligibility, how much weight will the IRS give it?

These types of deficiencies are likely to be the result of the whistleblower being unfamiliar with tax laws or the requirements of the IRS Reward Program. In addition, perhaps the whistleblower does not know how to calculate the loss or make the required allegations.

In some cases, the whistleblower does provide the required information, but the application itself is disorganized, poorly prepared, or inadequately presented. If you have specific proof of the amount of unpaid taxes, don't bury it in your application. Give it a separate heading, and then articulate, in a clear, concise, and complete manner, exactly how and why you believe the taxpayer underpaid taxes by an amount that exceeds $2 million. Remember, the standard is the amount of unpaid taxes, not the amount of undeclared income.

Other times, the whistleblower lacks enough information to prove the amount of unpaid taxes. What should you do, simply hope the IRS will issue subpoenas and figure out the tax loss? No. Rather than file the application with your fingers crossed in the hopes that the IRS may open an investigation and prove your suspicions, you should dig further before filing. There are no second chances. Wait to file the application until you can credibly demonstrate not only underpaid taxes, but the extent of the unpaid taxes.

Think about this issue in another way: If you cannot provide specific evidence of more than $2 million in unpaid taxes, what amount of reward do you realistically hope to receive? Fifteen percent of nothing is nothing.

The same is true for gathering evidence in support of the underlying allegations. The reward is for those who do the leg work, not simply alerting the IRS to potential tax evasion.

3. Facts are Too Speculative

The IRS will quickly reject applications that appear to be based on speculation. There are a variety of reasons why factual allegations lack the specificity to warrant the IRS opening a case.

Maybe the facts are just flat-out insufficient to state a claim, because the whistleblower does not have enough information to make the allegations. The manner in which the allegations are presented can also make the allegations appear vague, convoluted, or speculative, although the facts themselves are sufficient.

An example of speculation based upon insufficient facts will help clarify the situation. Suppose that Janell hires a large, successful painting company to paint her kitchen. The painters do great work, but when they are finished, they ask to be paid in cash. Janell is fairly confident that the company is making millions a year and suspects the company may be failing to report huge volumes of cash sales through its branches across the country. It may be true, but a busy IRS agent will rarely open investigations based upon one isolated instance or sale. On the other hand, if Janell were the bookkeeper for the company, knew their cash sales exceeded $6 million a year and could, in the course of her job, provide specific details of substantial cash sales going unreported, her claim will be much stronger.

A claim can also be deemed "too speculative" when the application just doesn't make sense. Perhaps the applicant used a shotgun approach, combining dozens of scattered allegations. If it looks chaotic and slapped together without careful thought, it won't make the top of the pile and risks being rejected outright. Be careful that your allegations do not sound like a mystery novel, because a busy agent lacks time to try to figure out "who did it."

As you think about filing an application, keep in mind that there are thousands of allegations of tax evasion reported to the IRS each year. It simply lacks resources to open cases where the allegations must substantially rely on speculation. The IRS is not interested in randomly issuing thousands of subpoenas each year to track down every potential tax evasion. Rather, the IRS is willing to pay sizeable rewards to those who have already researched the case sufficiently that they can provide the IRS with specific and detailed allegations.

Again, the IRS gets most excited when you have documents to support the allegations and the allegations clearly show why more than $2 million in taxes are owed.

It is inevitable that IRS agents will take most seriously the claims that are obviously professional, well informed, and thoroughly prepared.

4. Suspicious Motives or Family Squabbles

The fourth reason relates to suspicious motives. The IRS must dread applications that appear to be nothing more than family squabbles, with one side of a messy divorce trying to use the IRS as a weapon of vengeance. Of course, if the allegations involve a billionaire or other extremely wealthy individual, and the vengeful spouse can provide bank account information and documentation that their ex created an abusive trust, the IRS may still pursue the case. It would be a welcome exception to the general aversion IRS agents feel toward family squabbles.

The key point is that the IRS is interested in recovering unpaid taxes, not sorting out division of assets. Therefore, if you have specific, detailed, and credible information about unpaid taxes exceeding $2 million, the mere fact that the parties are related will not automatically eliminate your ability to receive a reward.

Conclusion

The IRS really does want to pay rewards. Most applications are rejected not because the IRS is fickle, but because the application fails to meet the technical requirements, is not specific, is too speculative, or is based on suspicious motives. These are all things within your control. Avoid them and you can formulate an application that will pass technical review.

Chapter Fourteen
Personal Risks of Reporting Tax Evasion

Be sure you put your feet in the right place, then stand firm.
— ABRAHAM LINCOLN (1809–1865)

It is only natural to ask questions such as: "What risks do I face?" "Will my name be made public?" "How much time and energy are required to earn a reward?"

Confidentiality

One of the biggest differences between the IRS Reward Program and the DOJ program on which it is modeled, is that the IRS does not need to disclose your name to the public in order to pay you a reward. In fact, the IRS prides itself on maintaining the confidentiality of its whistleblowers.

The IRS will not disclose your name to the tax cheater. However, there is one rare and limited circumstance in which this promise is not absolute.

The IRS can only pay rewards from amounts it recovers from a taxpayer who underpaid taxes. That makes sense. But what if the only way the IRS can prove tax evasion is through the *testimony* of the person filing for a reward? For instance, if the taxpayer shreds all of the relevant documents and the only way to prove the case is with your testimony about the tax scheme and that the person bragged to you about cheating, then the IRS may need to disclose your identity. Specifically, if the IRS could not reach a settlement, you may need to testify in Tax Court.

In the very rare instance that you are called to testify in court, your name will definitely be made public. The taxpayer will definitely learn that you are the one who reported him and filed a claim for a reward. Whenever you testify against the taxpayer, their attorney has the right to ask you questions, particularly about areas attorneys call "the potential for being biased." In other words, if you stand to gain 15% to 30% of what the IRS collects, the taxpayer's attorney will argue that you have a reason to be biased in your testimony and ask the court to discount what you say. Of course, the court is free to judge credibility and can accept every word you say as true. The point is, your name will be made known if you testify, though it is only a remote possibility that your testimony will be required.

The IRS will work with you in situations where it believes it needs your testimony and will discuss this with you before making a decision to call you as a witness. Of course, there is no way to know before-hand whether this situation will occur. The need for your testimony may not surface until sometime after you submit your application. You may be able to evaluate the odds somewhat. For instance, as you put together your application and describe the evidence, you should have a pretty good idea as to which documents exist and what other proof is available without your testimony.

The maintenance of secrecy also has a practical limitation. It's always possible that the tax cheater may simply guess that there was a whistleblower and that it was you, by a process of elimination.

In summary, the IRS will keep your name confidential in most cases. But it is only fair to tell you that there are no absolute guar-antees. The only way discloure of your identity may occur is the very rare case where you have to testify in order for the IRS to win and be able to pay you a reward. In addition, there can never be a guarantee that the tax cheater won't somehow figure out that you reported him to the IRS.

Time, Energy, and Patience

There are other forms of risk when claiming a reward. First, it can take a lot of time for you to earn a reward. It will require a big chunk of your time to gather and present the information to your attorney and the IRS. It often takes years for the IRS to prove tax evasion and collect the taxes due. You and your attorney may be asked to help the IRS understand and prove certain facts along the way.

The process also requires energy. Anytime you invest yourself into something, it takes emotional energy. You may be the type who worries or drifts off regularly into fantasy land about how to spend the reward. Either way, there is an emotional cost.

In addition, it may be difficult to remain patient. Because your whistleblower reward can only be paid out of actual proceeds collected by the IRS from the wrongdoer, you may feel like you are caught up in a waiting game. Again, it can take several years to get the reward. In the meantime, you will not be given any progress reports from the IRS.

Paying Taxes on Rewards

Not surprisingly, a whistleblower reward is taxable income. Whenever the IRS Whistleblower Office pays a reward, it issues to the whistleblower an IRS Form 1099. This form lists the full amount of the reward you received through the case. The form is also sent by the IRS Whistleblower Office to the appropriate department within the IRS that gathers forms from employers, banks, and others pertaining to income earned. That component of the IRS feeds this information into computers to ensure that all taxpayers are reporting these common sources of income on their tax returns.

Whistleblowers are generally allowed to deduct from income the amount of the contingency fees paid to their attorney. Thus, only the amount the whistleblower *receives* after paying the contingency fee should be taxable income. However, anytime you receive new and sizeable income, such as a reward, it is wise to consult with a tax accountant or advisor to makes sure you claim all available deductions.

Two Other Important Issues

Don't delay. Although not a risk *per se*, as discussed in prior chapters, you should act with deliberate speed when filing a reward application. Otherwise, you risk being barred because of the statute of limitation or being knocked out or receiving a reduced reward because someone else already filed the same claim.

Don't talk too much. Don't discuss your tax evasion allegations with anyone except your attorney. Again, be prepared for the IRS to pay less, if anything, to a person who files second. Don't risk someone else using your information to file a claim by talking to them about it.

Money Can't Buy Happiness

Many people play the lottery hoping to cash in so they can kiss their jobs goodbye. They dream of a blissful life that the winnings are supposed to provide. You may have similar goals in mind when dreaming about an IRS reward.

The truth is, your odds of receiving an IRS reward for a well-prepared application are vastly greater than your odds of winning the lottery. You may well receive millions of dollars for the right case. But I would feel remiss if I did not point out that money can't buy happiness.

If you were to interview everyone who received a million-dollar reward or big lottery jackpot, very few would say they are truly happier today. Reporting fraud may be the right thing to do, but that does not mean becoming rich will bring bliss, or even peace, to your life. There are simply greater things in life than wealth, such as family, country, and God.

Remain mindful that there is a high cost to be paid—certainly emotionally—for blowing the whistle on tax evasion. If you treat the case as a cheap lottery ticket, you won't invest the time and energy needed to present an application the IRS finds desirable. Often, the best cases are those of individuals who are seeking to right a wrong more so than obtain a reward. That type of motivation shows itself in the process by your determination.

In summary, weigh your decision carefully. Seek solid legal and practical advice from your attorney. In the end, however, the decision to file for a reward must be your own.

Reporting Tax Evasion Anonymously

If you decide that you do not want to go through the effort of claiming a reward, but still want to report federal income tax fraud, you can contact the IRS directly. In fact, the IRS permits, and even encourages, citizens to report tax evasion without claiming a reward. Because you are not claiming a reward, you can do so anonymously.

If you do report the case anonymously, you may still be able to change your mind and claim a reward later, but there will be some obstacles. For instance, if another person files before you do, you may not be able to leapfrog ahead of them, even if you made the first anonymous tip. Your initial report may also provoke a public disclosure or a settlement before you can prepare your application and claim your reward.

If it is your desire to alert the IRS without claiming a reward, you can get information about doing so from the IRS website. The IRS has a web page named, "How Do You Report Suspected Tax Fraud Activity?" To get there, first, go to *www.IRS.gov*. Toward the top of the page is the search term box. Type in the term "how to report fraud" or even the entire phrase, "How Do You Report Suspected Tax Fraud Activity." After you click search, the website will list a link to that page. Just follow the instructions and you can easily report suspected tax evasion.

If you want to report fraud, waste, or abuse to the Treasury Inspector General for Tax Administration (TIGTA), or if you want to confidentially report misconduct, waste, fraud, or abuse by an IRS employee or a tax professional, you can call 1-800-366-4484 (1-800-877-8339 for TTY/TDD users). (The IRS reports directly to the Department of Treasury, so it is answerable to that agency.)

Conclusion

One of the best attributes of the IRS Reward Program is that, in most cases, your name will never be disclosed, even if you receive a reward. By contrast, the worst part of the IRS Reward Program is that the IRS will provide you with little, if any, information during its investigative process or afterward. The fact that it often takes years before you either are paid a reward or told that your claim was rejected is a close second.

If you can stomach these drawbacks and are prepared to spend time digging for information and preparing your application, there are a lot of good reasons to step forward—including doing the right thing and helping to ensure that everyone carries their own weight in paying the taxes needed for many valuable government programs.

Chapter Fifteen

A Checklist to Follow

Doing what's right isn't the problem. It is knowing what's right.
— Lyndon B. Johnson (1908–1973)

This chapter provides you with a preliminary checklist to help you evaluate whether you have a tax evasion case worth reporting. It also outlines the confidential questionnaire many attorneys use when screening cases. It will help you organize the information to give to an attorney, who can then carefully evaluate the allegations. By reading through this chapter, you will have a good idea of what the attorney will ask of you when you first consult him.

A Checklist to Follow

It is no secret that many companies and individuals are cheating on their taxes. The amount is surprising, as high as 15%, and results in as much as $350 billion in unpaid taxes each year.

The IRS wants to involve you, but only if you can present a solid claim of an underpayment of taxes. Remember that the following mini-checklists do not provide legal advice and are not a substitute for asking an experienced attorney to review your particular facts and circumstances. However, they can assist you in making the important decision of whether to report tax evasion.

Step One: Find Out If You Meet the Requirements

Can you meet the statutory requirements using the *Four F Factor* criteria for tax evasion cases? It is time to find out.

As outlined in Chapter Six, the *Four F Factors* consist of:

Filing first
Format is fundamentally correct
Federal tax funds unpaid
Funds are forfeited.

Below, these four factors are highlighted, followed by a checklist for you to work through.

First to File. Timing matters. It is always best to be the first one to file for a reward. If someone else already filed, your reward, if any, will be much less unless you bring something new to the table. If the allegations had already been publicly disclosed, you have some additional hurdles to address.

Format. This encompasses a lot of different elements. Obviously, it includes filling out Form 211 and signing the declaration stating under penalty of perjury that the information is true. If you are serious about the case and have based your claim on solid evidence, this should not be a problem. However, the informal formatting issues are what really matter. You should submit a compelling memo in support of the allegations to gain the attention of the IRS, as discussed in Chapter Ten. If your allegations are not specific, detailed, and credible, you have little chance of receiving a significant reward. In fact, the IRS is not likely to even open an investigation.

Federal Taxes Owed. To be eligible for a reward under the new program, you must be able to show at least $2 million in unpaid taxes. This amount can be estimated using the $6 million rule of thumb. You should be able to establish a total of $6 million in unallowable deductions or income not reported. This will be a deciding factor in whether the IRS opens a case and in determining how much of a reward you may receive. And if the claim is against an individual, the person must also have earned at least $200,000 in gross taxable income in one relevant year.

If you do not meet these threshold amounts, you are still technically eligible for a reward under the old program rules. But, those cases are not as likely to be received with enthusiasm or pay significant rewards.

Funds Forfeited. Rewards are paid out of the funds the IRS actually recovers from the taxpayer based upon your allegations. Therefore, you should give some consideration as to whether the taxpayer has liquid assets to be able to pay the IRS or if they are in bankruptcy. If it is likely that the IRS will not collect a significant amount, your reward may be too small to warrant the effort.

The following sections contain two checklists, which not only address these four factors, but also include a formula for preparing to file your application.

Checklist One

1. Will I sign a declaration? . . . . Yes ☐ No ☐ Not sure ☐
2. Did they underpay taxes by
   $2 million? . . . . Yes ☐ No ☐ Not sure ☐
3. If an individual, did he earn
   $200,000? . . . . Yes ☐ No ☐ Not sure ☐
4. Do I have proof of a tax
   underpayment? . . . . Yes ☐ No ☐ Not sure ☐
5. Am I the first to file? . . . . Yes ☐ No ☐ Not sure ☐

Evaluation of Checklist

If you answer no to question one, you cannot apply for a reward. Again, you must use your real name and sign Form 211.

If you answered no to questions two and three, this may not be the right case to file. Please carefully re-read Chapter Six regarding the threshold dollar amounts and how they are calculated. If you do not meet them, don't waste your time. *This is the single most common error made by applicants.* Because the IRS receives so many claims below the requirement of $2 million in "unpaid taxes," you need to clearly state in your application the estimated amount and how you calculated it. You do not want your application dismissed because it looked like a run-of-the-mill claim that does not meet the threshold.

In addition, if your claim alleges that an individual underpaid taxes (as opposed to a company), be sure that you include a statement that they earned more than $200,000 in one of the years at issue. Although Form 211 does not ask for this information, it is a requirement that must be established, so you should include it in your statement of material evidence attached to your application. You do not want the IRS presuming that you cannot meet this requirement. Don't trust that the IRS will simply assume that the taxpayer must have earned that amount; tell the IRS why you contend they did. The last thing you want is a clerk making a quick review of your application and attachments only to conclude that a technical requirement was not met and have your claim rejected before the heart of the allegations are even considered.

Question four is more of a rhetorical question. Do not file until you can answer yes. The key to a winning application is not only possessing specific and detailed information, but effectively communicating that to the IRS. As stressed throughout this book, you really should submit a detailed statement of material support for your allegations. Simply filling out the IRS form will not guarantee that your application will receive the attention it deserves. It is vital that you completely explain why the taxpayer underpaid taxes, including the proof, and attach any key documents you possess.

Question five is trickier. It is difficult to disprove that someone else filed first, so an uncertain answer there may not be significant. Again, the IRS has not stated that you cannot receive a reward if you are second in line. But being second does significantly and negatively affect your chance of receiving a reward. In fact, just the thought of another person filing before you should make you feel a lump in your throat. The best case scenario would be if the IRS pays rewards in proportion to what it perceives as the value added by a second in time application. In any event, you will not know whether someone has filed before you. Thus, the best strategy is to proceed deliberately and avoid being second.

If you are unsure of some answers, it does not mean that you don't have a case worth pursuing. Rather, you need to be up front with yourself and your attorney on these points. Consider whether you can take any steps to improve your chances or whether it may not be worth the time and effort.

Step Two: Check Statute of Limitation

The biggest concern is often the age of the case. Does it safely fall within the three-year general statute of limitation (SOL)? In those instances, you only need to show that taxes are owed; you don't have to worry about whether the taxpayer intended to cheat. The same is true for the few types of matters governed by the six-year statute of limitation, as explained in Chapter Eight.

On the other hand, there is no statute of limitation when you are able to show that the taxpayer knew they were committing tax fraud. In those instances, the IRS must prove the taxpayer intended to cheat by clear and convincing evidence. This is a fancy way of saying that a judge or jury needs to be reasonably certain. This is a much higher burden of proof than a standard case within the statute of limitation. In those instances, the IRS must only convince the court by a preponderance of the evidence, which simply means it is more likely than not.

In other words, the standard burden is to show that it is more likely than not that the person owes taxes. If you were to try to put percentages to these legal terms, the normal case is 51% sure, where as to prove fraud by clear and convincing evidence you would need to be 65% sure, which starts approaching the standard in a criminal case requiring proof beyond a reasonable doubt. Thus, in older cases, you really should have a smoking gun document or direct testimony from a credible witness who can testify that the taxpayer admitted it was cheating. Otherwise, the IRS may not bother with an old case where the deck is stacked against it.

Although the standard is very high for old cases, the reward can be enormous if you show fraud. The key point is that a busy IRS agent doesn't like stale cases, but loves any case, even if it is six years old, where you have lots of credible proof of tax fraud.

Next, if the allegations already were the subject of a public disclosure, such as a newspaper article or published government report, you will need to show that you fit the requirements of an "original source," as discussed in Chapter Seven. If you can meet the exception, you are still entitled to a reward of up to 30%. Otherwise, your reward will be capped at 10% and could even be zero.

Checklist Two

Are underpayments older than
   3 years? .... Yes ☐   No ☐   Not sure ☐
If so, does the 6 year SOL apply? ... Yes ☐   No ☐   Not sure ☐
If outside the 3 or 6 year SOL,
   can I show intent to defraud?..... Yes ☐   No ☐   Not sure ☐
Was the allegation publicly
   disclosed? .... Yes ☐   No ☐   Not sure ☐
If so, am I the original source of
   the information?.............. Yes ☐   No ☐   Not sure ☐

Evaluation of Checklist

The IRS program does not state that you must prove fraud to collect a reward, although it definitely will be more excited if you can prove tax fraud. The IRS Reward Program is broad enough to include mere underpayment of taxes. However, there are very strict "statute of limitation" rules—which is three years for most cases.

Again, it is important to remember that there is no statute of limitation when you are able to show that the taxpayer knew they were committing tax fraud. The IRS looks at a fraud case entirely differently. It can pursue any case where it can prove the person or company knew it was cheating. Of course, there are practical realities in proving an old case. If you have a smoking gun document or admission by the taxpayer that they knew they were cheating, by all means file an older case. If not, it is an uphill battle that may not be worth the effort.

In terms of public disclosure, it is fairly easy to find out if there has been a prior disclosure in the media. Although it will not be conclusive, begin by conducting an Internet search of the person or company and add the search term "taxes." Try it again with the term "fraud." You get the idea. Try several searches using words that relate to your allegations.

If you answered yes to the public disclosure question, you will need to have a frank discussion with your attorney, preferably one with experience with whistleblower reward programs. He will need to evaluate whether the public disclosure bar actually applies, which eliminates or greatly reduces the amount of your potential reward. Your attorney should also be able to assess whether you meet the so-called original source exception, which could lift you back into the 15% to 30% range of a reward.

There is one key factor in your favor; the taxpayer is not allowed to raise the issue of the public disclosure bar or file a motion to exclude you from receiving a reward. However, this does not reduce the importance of relying upon legal counsel and making a convincing argument that you meet the requirements. Remember, you only get one shot at convincing the IRS of your status. But once you do, you are nearly home free. The taxpayer is not allowed to second guess or become involved in the process. It is an issue solely between you and the IRS.

Step Three: Select Your Attorney

Assuming your checklists helped you decide that you appear to have a good case, the final step is deciding whether to use an attorney, and if so, selecting your attorney. If you decide to file yourself instead, put your best foot forward by following all of the strategies in this book.

If you want to use an attorney, how do you select one? It is important to make a good selection because your attorney's efforts in presenting your application to the IRS will be a big factor in how the IRS perceives your case and whether it gets the attention it deserves. If you open the yellow pages section of a telephone book, there are hundreds—even thousands—of attorneys. How do you decide which one is right for you?

You should choose an attorney based upon a combination of their legal ability and whatever personal attributes are important to you. The attorney you choose should also be admitted to the U.S. Tax Court in Washington, D.C., which is the place where any appeals must be filed.

The attorney you hire must be able to properly evaluate your case, present a convincing application that meets all of the requirements in the statute and work well with the government. Plan to ask those you consider about their experience with whistleblower reward programs. Just as you would not want your family doctor to perform your heart surgery, you may not want a general practice attorney to handle your reward application.

With respect to personal qualities, this is a subjective determination made through individual preferences. Be sure to hire an attorney you are comfortable interacting with. Ask yourself if you feel confident that he will keep you informed and treat you with the appropriate concern and care. You will be working with him for several years, so select someone who is compatible with your personality.

After you have made your selection, put your trust in your attorney. Don't second-guess him. Although you can expect to be informed of any significant events, do not expect weekly reports. Reread this book to keep the long-term perspective in mind: You and your attorney are working toward a goal. It will take time and perseverance.

If you are not able to locate an attorney experienced with government reward programs, is it better to file by yourself or use an attorney that has little or no experience with reward programs?

That is a tough call. You must judge whether the skills the attorney brings to the table is worth the 40% to 50% of any reward. At the same time, you only get one shot, so you need to hit the bull's eye. If you are confident in your ability to clearly organize and articulate your claim, as addressed in Chapter Ten, it improves your chances. Only you can judge whether you are better off to hire an attorney.

Finally, remember, these checklists are not legal advice. Experienced legal counsel with knowledge of your allegations is most qualified to discuss your circumstances and evaluate your potential case.

Step Four: Fill Out the Questionnaire

If you are serious about reporting tax evasion, you should be willing to answer a detailed questionnaire to provide your attorney with the facts he needs. Most law firms that specialize in representing whistleblowers have their own version of a questionnaire, which is often referred to as an "intake form." Many times, the questionnaire is on their website and you are asked to fill it out before discussing your potential case.

Remember, however, that a questionnaire is just an initial screening tool. It is a beginning point for organizing your allegations and helping your attorney to effectively gather more information.

After you complete the intake form, and you agree to hire the attorney and he agrees to represent you, then you will be asked to sign a retainer agreement formalizing the attorney-client relationship. Afterwards, a lengthy interview will be conducted to gather the specific details needed to properly prepare a memorandum in support of the allegations to attach to Form 211.

Even though you will be interviewed later, filling out the initial questionnaire will not be a waste of time. Your attorney will later ask you many of the questions on the form. If you have taken the time to answer them at your leisure, it will be much easier to answer them in a live interview later.

Below is a sample questionnaire concerning tax evasion. As you consider how to answer these questions, be guided by these three principles:

1. Be truthful, without exaggerating.
2. Speak up, if you don't know or are not sure about something.
3. Provide as much detail as possible.

When answering the more detailed questions on an intake form—such as, describing the tax evasion scheme or your evidence in support—plan to write several paragraphs.

Before you begin, note that attorneys vary regarding whether they ask you to include the name of the company or individuals engaged in tax evasion at this preliminary stage. Some attorneys ask the potential client not to disclose names of the person or company you allege underpaid taxes until after an initial inquiry is made; thus, you do not identify them in the questionnaire. Other attorneys ask for the names of those underpaying taxes upfront and you can tell them when they ask. Both approaches are acceptable.

In any event, the primary purpose of an intake form is to allow your potential attorney to initially gauge the nature, size, and strength of your case. Often, your answers will reveal a technical requirement that cannot be overcome, and prevent you from wasting time. Other times, it shows weaknesses that need to be developed to strengthen your case.

In addition, your responses will facilitate any future discussion with your attorney. After he reviews your form, he will contact you for more details if he thinks you have a potential case in which he may represent you.

It is time to begin. Plan to answer the following questionnaire or intake form.

Confidential Questionnaire for Tax Fraud

1. Are the allegations that a company underpaid taxes? (Yes or no)
2. Are the allegations that an individual underpaid taxes? (Yes or no)
3. If the allegations are that an individual underpaid taxes, did the person have at least $200,000 in gross taxable income during one of the tax years in question? (Yes or no)
4. Was the amount of underpayment of taxes $2 million or more? (Yes or no)
5. How much money did the taxpayer underpay on their taxes, and describe how you calculated or estimated the amount? (Please break down the amounts by years.)
6. If you contend that the taxpayer intentionally cheated, explain how and why. (Please include the evidence you have to support that they knew they were cheating.)
7. How did you become aware of the underpayment of taxes?
8. Do you have any documents to help prove the allegations? (If so, briefly describe them.)
9. When did the underpayment of taxes occur? (Please state which years, when it stopped, and whether it is still going on.)
10. If the allegations are against a company, did you once work for the company? (Yes or no)
11. If the allegations are against a company, do you now work for the company? (Yes or no)

12. Have you already told the person or company that you thought they underpaid taxes? (Yes or no)

13. Have your allegations been the subject of any legal action or newspaper story, or have the allegations been disclosed in any lawsuit, agency hearing, congressional hearing, or government audit? If so, briefly describe them.

14. Have you talked to another attorney about this matter? (Yes or no)

15. I have read and agree with these statements:

Although we will treat the information confidential, the transmission of any information is not intended to create, and receipt does not constitute, an attorney-client relationship. Even if you submit the questionnaire to me, that does not make me your lawyer. Instead, we will use your information to investigate the matter and to determine whether we can and will represent you in bringing your whistleblower case. Only when we both sign a written agreement will we actually become your lawyer and advocate. A fraud case can take a number of years from start to finish and it can be expensive for a lawyer to take a case. Therefore, we conduct a thorough analysis of cases and we do not accept every case. It may take time to evaluate your questionnaire, and we may be busy on other matters at the time you send your questionnaire. If our time constraints do not fit your needs, you may wish to discuss your matter with another attorney.

How the Attorney Uses This Information

When filling out this information, you may be wondering how the attorney will use the information. You want to know if it is safe to provide specific details right now, before you sign a retainer agreement. Relax. You are in safe hands.

The first thing to know is that all attorneys must treat your responses as confidential. Even though a formal attorney-client relationship does not yet exist, by law, all preliminary discussions with an attorney, while you are in the process of selecting an attorney, are as privileged as those after you sign a formal retainer agreement hiring counsel. This means that regardless of whether you select a particular attorney, the attorney cannot use your information for their personal use or disclose it to others.

The attorney will examine your preliminary explanations of the allegations to determine what issues are most important. For instance, is there an issue concerning the statute of limitation that needs to be explored?

Each question in the questionnaire is very important and helps the attorney frame the meeting with the potential client. Therefore, plan to provide more, not less, information.

There are times when a person states that the allegations clearly do not meet the technical requirements, such as being under $2 million, and the attorney will simply inform the person that they are declining to take the case and stating the basic reasons. It may not be possible to have a second chance when filing your claim with the IRS, but you do have an opportunity to ask questions and get specific information while choosing your attorney. If you think the attorney is wrong to reject your case, you can either provide more information to that attorney or seek a second opinion.

Conclusion

Before you file a reward application, you need to spend time evaluating your case. Actually working through the checklists and answering the sample questionnaire will help you decide whether you have a good case or if you need to gather more information. It is important to put your best foot forward at every step of the process, beginning with contacting an attorney through submitting a high quality intake form.

Chapter Sixteen
Conclusion

Truth will ultimately prevail where there is pains to bring it to light.
— GEORGE WASHINGTON (1732–1799)

Roughly 15% of federal taxes are underpaid each year. This amounts to annual losses of $350 billion to the federal government. If those funds are not recovered from those cheating, that money must be made up by the remaining 85% of honest taxpayers, costing more than $1,000 per taxpayer.

For those cheating on their taxes, the threat of random IRS audits has lost it sting. It has become apparent that the government lacks resources to conduct the audits necessary to stem the immense losses. Less than 2% of all tax returns are audited, not even scratching the surface of the amount of unpaid taxes. More and more people are finding that they can get away with cheating the government because there simply are not enough government officials and resources to keep everyone honest.

Fortunately, the government finally discovered a new and necessary strategy to stop the voluminous cheating: rewarding private citizens for becoming watchdogs. In a program built upon the proverb "a worker is worth his wages,"[12] Congress mandated that the IRS revamp its old Informant Program and start paying rewards of up to 30% to the citizens reporting underpaid taxes.

The IRS is standing by, waiting and even inviting you to join in. If and when good cases are submitted by whistleblowers, the new

IRS Reward Program could pay over $100 billion in rewards each year. That means there are many opportunities for you, the honest taxpayer, to receive a sizeable reward.

All that glitters is not gold, however. It is important to know what type of case is eligible and how to assess whether your particular case is worth filing. It could cripple the IRS Whistleblower Office if thousands of people dashed to send applications that contain little evidence and even less hope of recovery.

That is why you must carefully evaluate what you believe to be underpaid taxes. While timing is important, make sure you critically look at the situation you want to report. Does it satisfy all of the technical requirements? Have you discussed possible public disclosures with an attorney? Are you prepared, mentally and emotionally, to enter into a process that could take six years? Are you dedicated to the process and able to keep your eyes on the goal?

This book fulfills its two purposes: First, to communicate the workings of the new IRS Reward Program, so that you, a member of the public, will know how to obtain the rewards Congress has authorized for you. Second, and equally important, to describe the program in sufficient detail so that you know when *not* to file for a reward.

If you discover that your case is not worth reporting, it would be a shame for you to waste your time and energy on a case that would not produce a reward or any unpaid taxes. But if you learn that you have a potentially winning case, this book has given you the tools to begin the process of receiving a sizable reward by assisting the government in recovering millions of dollars. If the right case comes along, you could benefit from a reward as high as $1 billion.

Because the IRS Reward Program is new and continues to develop, *www.HowToReportFraud.com,* the author's website, is regularly updated and expanded with additional resources that will help you report tax evasion.

Best wishes in your efforts to collect your government reward as you report tax evasion (or report other fraud against the government under the related DOJ Reward Program).

Endnotes

Chapter Two
2   DOJ Press Release *(http://www.usdoj.gov/criminal/npftf/pr/press_ releases/2008/nov/11-10-08_frd-fls-clam-fy08.pdf)*.

Chapter Three
3   "Treasury Inspector General for Tax Administration, The Informant's Rewards Program Needs More Centralized Management Oversight" (June 2006) *http://www.ustreas.gov/ tigta/auditreports/2006reports/200630092fr.pdf.*

4   Ibid.

Chapter Four
5   "IRS Deals FedEx a Setback on Classification of Workers" *http://online.wsj.com/article/SB119827792153645881. html?mod=googlenews_wsj.*

6   "Independent Contractor: Self-Employed or Employee?" *http://www.irs.gov/businesses/small/article/0,,id=99921,00.html* (The IRS also has a bulletin to help a company determine the answer: *http://www.irs.gov/taxtopics/tc762.html*).

Chapter Five
7   "Senate Report Examines Role of Banks in Tax Evasion," *New York Times* (July 17, 2008) *http://www.nytimes.com/2008/ 07/17/washington/17tax.html.*

8   "Tax Cheats Cost Americans $100 Billion, Senate Report Says Offshore Tax Abuses May Cost U.S. $100 Billion a Year," *Money* (July 17, 2008) *http://money.cnn.com/2008/07/17/news/tax_ evasion.ap/index.htm?postversion=2008071704.*

Chapter Seven

9 *Allison Engine Co., Inc. v. U.S. ex rel. Sanders*, 128 S. Ct. 2123 (2008). The author wrote a series of law review articles outlining the original source exception and proposing standards for the courts to follow. They are located on the author's website at: *http://www. HowToReportFraud.com.*

Chapter Eight

10 *Badaracco v. C.I.R.*, 464 U.S. 386 (1984).

Chapter Twelve

11 See Appendix E.

Chapter Sixteen

12 Based upon 1 Timothy 5:18 ("The worker deserves his wages.") (New International Version).

Appendices

IRS Reward Statute (Codifying the IRS Whistleblower Reward Program: 26 U.S.C. § 7623)

26 U.S.C.A. § 7623/I.R.C. § 7623
Title 26. Internal Revenue Code (Refs & Annos)

Subtitle F. Procedure and Administration (Refs & Annos)
Chapter 78. Discovery of Liability and Enforcement of Title
Subchapter B. General Powers and Duties
§ 7623. Expenses of detection of underpayments and fraud, etc.

(a) In general.—The Secretary, under regulations prescribed by the Secretary, is authorized to pay such sums as he deems necessary for—
    (1) detecting underpayments of tax, or
    (2) detecting and bringing to trial and punishment persons guilty of violating the internal revenue laws or conniving at the same, in cases where such expenses are not otherwise provided for by law. Any amount payable under the preceding sentence shall be paid from the proceeds of amounts collected by reason of the information provided, and any amount so collected shall be available for such payments.

(b) Awards to whistleblowers.—

    (1) In general.—If the Secretary proceeds with any administrative or judicial action described in subsection (a) based on information brought to the Secretary's attention by an individual, such individual shall, subject to paragraph (2), receive as an award at least 15 percent but not more than 30 percent of the collected proceeds (including penalties, interest, additions to tax, and additional amounts) resulting from the action (including any related actions) or from any settlement in response to such action. The determination of the amount of such award by the Whistleblower Office shall depend upon the extent to which the individual substantially contributed to such action.

    (2) Award in case of less substantial contribution.—

        (A) In general.—In the event the action described in paragraph (1) is one which the Whistleblower Office determines to be based principally on disclosures of specific allegations (other than information provided by the individual described in paragraph (1)) resulting from a judicial or administrative hearing, from a governmental report, hearing, audit, or investigation, or from the news media, the Whistleblower Office may award such sums as it considers appropriate, but in no case more than 10 percent of the collected proceeds (including penalties, interest, additions to tax, and additional amounts) resulting from the action (including any related actions) or from any settlement in response to such action, taking into account the significance of the individual's information and the role of such individual and any legal representative of such individual in contributing to such action.

        (B) Nonapplication of paragraph where individual is original source of information.—Subparagraph (A) shall not apply if the information resulting in the initiation of the action described in paragraph (1) was originally provided by the individual described in paragraph (1).

(3) Reduction in or denial of award.—If the Whistleblower Office determines that the claim for an award under paragraph (1) or (2) is brought by an individual who planned and initiated the actions that led to the underpayment of tax or actions described in subsection (a)(2), then the Whistleblower Office may appropriately reduce such award. If such individual is convicted of criminal conduct arising from the role described in the preceding sentence, the Whistleblower Office shall deny any award.

(4) Appeal of award determination.—Any determination regarding an award under paragraph (1), (2), or (3) may, within 30 days of such determination, be appealed to the Tax Court (and the Tax Court shall have jurisdiction with respect to such matter).

(5) Application of this subsection.—This subsection shall apply with respect to any action—

> **(A)** against any taxpayer, but in the case of any individual, only if such individual's gross income exceeds $200,000 for any taxable year subject to such action, and

> **(B)** if the tax, penalties, interest, additions to tax, and additional amounts in dispute exceed $2,000,000.

(6) Additional rules.—

> **(A) No contract necessary.**—No contract with the Internal Revenue Service is necessary for any individual to receive an award under this subsection.

> **(B) Representation.**—Any individual described in paragraph (1) or (2) may be represented by counsel.

> **(C) Submission of information.**—No award may be made under this subsection based on information submitted to the Secretary unless such information is submitted under penalty of perjury.

Appendix B

IRS Guidance (Effective as of January 14, 2008)

Part III—Administrative, Procedural, and Miscellaneous
Claims Submitted to the IRS Whistleblower Office under
Section 7623
Notice 2008-4

SECTION 1. PURPOSE

This Notice provides guidance to the public on how to file claims under Internal Revenue Code section 7623 as amended by the Tax Relief and Health Care Act of 2006, Pub. L. No. 109-432 (120 Stat. 2958) (the Act) enacted on December 20, 2006.

SECTION 2. BACKGROUND

Section 406 of the Act amended section 7623 of the Internal Revenue Code concerning the payment of awards to certain persons who detect underpayments of tax. Prior statutory authority to pay awards at the discretion of the Secretary was re-designated as section 7623(a), and a new section 7623(b) was added to the Code. Additional provisions in section 406 of the Act establish a Whistleblower Office within the IRS and address reward program administration issues. These provisions were not incorporated into the Code.

The award program authorized by section 7623(a) has been previously implemented through regulations appearing at section

301.7623-1 of the Procedure and Administration Regulations, the substance of which is reprinted as IRS Publication 733, with additional administrative guidance appearing in the Internal Revenue Manual. Those regulations and Internal Revenue Manual provisions will continue to be followed for award claims within the scope of section 7623(a), except to the extent Sections 3.02 and 3.03 of this Notice provides interim guidance regarding submissions of information under section 7623(a).

New section 7623(b) requires that awards be made for submissions meeting certain criteria. Individuals are eligible for section 7623(b) awards based on the amount collected as a result of any administrative or judicial action resulting from the information provided. Because new section 7623(b) includes several requirements that are inconsistent with existing regulations and administrative guidance applicable to award claims under section 7623(a), the regulations which appear at section 301.7623-1 will not apply to the new award program authorized by section 7623(b). This Notice provides interim guidance applicable to award claims submitted under the authority of section 7623(b). In addition, this Notice seeks public comment on the topics covered herein.

SECTION 3.   INTERIM GUIDANCE

3.01 Eligibility Requirements to Submit Claims Under Section 7623(b)

To be eligible for an award under section 7623(b), the tax, penalties, interest, additions to tax, and additional amounts in dispute must exceed in the aggregate $2,000,000 and, if the allegedly noncompliant person is an individual, the individual's gross income must exceed $200,000 for any taxable year at issue in a claim. If the thresholds in section 7623(b) are not met, section 7623(a) authorizes, but does not require, the Service to pay for information relating to violations of the internal revenue laws that result in the government's recovery of tax. Submissions that do not qualify under section 7623(b) will be processed under section 7623(a). Unlike payments made on claims under section 7623(b), there is no requirement that payments made on claims under section 7623(a) be subject to the statutory award percentages. The United States Tax

Court appeal provisions added by the Act and codified in section 7623(b)(4) are applicable exclusively to award claims under section 7623(b). Accordingly, there is no right to appeal to the Tax Court for claims under section 7623(a).

3.02. Submission of Information for Award under Sections 7623(a) or (b)

(1) Individuals submitting information under section 7623(a) or (b) must complete IRS Form 211, Application for Award for Original Information (available on *www.irs.gov*) and send the completed Form 211 to:

> Internal Revenue Service
> Whistleblower Office
> SE:WO
> 1111 Constitution Ave., N.W.
> Washington, D.C. 20224

(2) All claims for awards must be submitted under penalty of perjury in accordance with section 3.03(9) below.

Until further guidance is issued, claims for awards may not be submitted electronically or by fax.

3.03 Information to be Included with IRS Form 211.

The Form 211 must be completed in its entirety and should include the following information:

(1) The date the claimant submits the claim;

(2) Claimant's name;

(3) Name of claimant's spouse (if applicable);

(4) Claimant's contact information, including address with zip code and telephone number;

(5) Claimant's date of birth;

(6) Claimant's Taxpayer Identification Number (e.g., Social Security Number or Individual Taxpayer Identification Number) and Taxpayer Identification Number of claimant's spouse, if applicable.

(7) Specific and credible information concerning the person(s) that the claimant believes have failed to comply with tax laws and

which will lead to the collection of unpaid taxes. This information should include the following:

 (i) The legal name of the person(s) (e.g., individual or entity), and any related person(s), that committed the violation of tax laws;

 (ii) The person's aliases, if any;

 (iii) The person's address;

 (iv) The person's Taxpayer Identification Number(s);

 (v) A description of the amount(s) and tax year(s) of Federal tax claimed to be owed, and facts supporting the basis for the amount(s) claimed to be owed;

 (vi) Documentation to substantiate the claim (e.g., financial data; the location of bank accounts, assets, books, and records; transaction documents or analyses relevant to the claim); and

 (vii) Any and all other facts and information pertaining to the claim.

If available information is not provided by the claimant, the claimant bears the risk that such information may not be considered by the Whistleblower Office in making any award determination. If documents or supporting evidence are known to the claimant but are not in his or her possession or control, the claimant should describe these documents and identify their location to the best of his or her ability.

(8) Explanation of how the information that forms the basis of the claim came to the attention of the claimant, including the date(s) on which this information was acquired, and a complete description of the claimant's present or former relationship (if any) to the person that is the subject of the claim (e.g., family member, acquaintance, client, employee, accountant, lawyer, bookkeeper, customer). If the claimant identifies multiple person(s) as the subject of a claim, describe his or her relationship to each person.

(9) Information submitted under section 7623 must be accompanied by an original signed declaration under penalty of perjury, as follows:

I declare, under penalty of perjury, that I have examined this application and my accompanying statement and supporting documentation and aver that such application is true, correct and complete, to the best of my knowledge.

The requirement to submit information under penalty of perjury precludes submissions by: (1) a person serving as a representative of the claimant, or (2) an entity other than a natural person. With respect to claims under section 7623(b), the requirement to submit information under penalty of perjury precludes submissions made anonymously or under an alias.

(10) Joint claims must be signed by each claimant and each claimant must sign the claim under penalty of perjury as described in 3.03(8).

3.04 Examples of Grounds for not Processing Claims Under Section 7623(b)

Examples of claims that will not be processed under section 7623(b) include:

(1) Claims submitted by an individual who is an employee of the Department of Treasury, or who is acting within the scope of his/her duties as an employee of any Federal, State, or local Government.

(2) Claims submitted by an individual who is required by Federal law or regulation to disclose the information, or by an individual who is precluded by Federal law or regulation from making the disclosure.

(3) Claims submitted by an individual who obtained or was furnished the information while acting in an official capacity as a member of a State body or commission having access to such materials as Federal returns, copies or abstracts.

(4) Claims submitted by an individual who had access to taxpayer information arising out of a contract with the Federal government that forms the basis of the claim.

(5) Claims that upon initial review have no merit or that lack sufficient specific and credible information.

(6) Claims submitted anonymously or under an alias.

(7) Claims filed by a person other than a natural person (such as a corporation or a partnership).

(8) The alleged noncompliant person is an individual whose gross income is below $200,000 for all taxable years at issue in a claim.

3.05 Acknowledgment of Claim by Whistleblower Office

The Whistleblower Office will acknowledge receipt of a claim in writing. If required information has not been submitted on a Form 211, the Whistleblower Office may return a Form 211 to the claimant for completion and submission. Following submission of the claim, the Whistleblower Office may, in its sole discretion, offer the opportunity to confer with the claimant to discuss the claim to ensure that the Service fully understands the information submitted with the claim. The Whistleblower Office, in its sole discretion, may ask for additional assistance from the claimant or any legal representative of such individual. Any assistance shall be under the direction and control of the Whistleblower Office or the office assigned to investigate the matter. The submission of a claim does not create an agency relationship between the claimant and the Federal Government, nor does the claimant act in any way on behalf of the Federal Government.

3.06 Confidentiality of Claimant's Identity

The Service will protect the identity of the claimant to the fullest extent permitted by law. Under some circumstances, such as when the claimant is needed as a witness in a judicial proceeding, it may not be possible to pursue the investigation or examination without revealing the claimant's identity. The Service will make every effort to inform the claimant before proceeding in such a case.

3.07 IRS Process for Evaluating Claim

The process for evaluating a claim is initiated by Service consideration of the information provided by the claimant in light of the facts developed by the Service in investigating the claim. This process will also consider whether the information submitted by the claimant resulted in administrative action taken by the Service or judicial action. For example, in the case of large entities where the entities' tax returns are subject to annual examination by the Service, an administrative action can mean the creation of a new issue under the Audit Plan or a change in the way information about an issue is collected or analyzed, which would not otherwise have occurred without the information provided by the claimant. In other cases, an administrative action may include initiating an examination of the person which would not otherwise have occurred without information provided by the claimant. Alternatively, a claimant's description of information when the alleged noncompliant person is already under investigation and when the information results in no change in the manner regarding how the issue is approached or resolved would not generally be regarded as resulting in administrative or judicial action and therefore would not be eligible for an award.

3.08 Duration of Process from Submitted Claim to Award Determination.

The process, from submission of complete information to the Service until the proceeds that serve as the basis for any award determination are collected, may take several years. Accordingly, the Service is unable to make any commitment to the claimant concerning the expected duration of the process.

Payment of awards will not be made until there is a final determination of the tax liability (including taxes, penalties, interest, additions to tax and additional amounts) owed to the Service and such amounts have been collected by the Service. Examples of when a final determination of tax liability can be made include, but are not limited to: (1) at the administrative level, when the Service and person that is the subject of the claimant's allegations enter into a closing agreement which conclusively waives the right to appeal or otherwise challenge a deficiency or additional tax liability determined by the Service; (2) if the person that is the subject of the claimant's allegations petitions the United States Tax Court for a redetermination of a deficiency, when the decision in that case becomes final within the meaning of section 7481; and (3) after the expiration of the statutory period for a taxpayer to file a claim for refund and to file a refund suit based on that claim against the United States or, if a refund suit is filed, when the judgment in that suit becomes final. In a case in which litigation is commenced, any award consideration will be delayed until that litigation has been concluded with finality.

3.09 Percentages Applied to Awards Under 7623(b)

The Whistleblower Office will make the final determination whether an award will be paid and the amount of the award for claims which it processes. Awards will be paid in proportion to the value of information furnished voluntarily with respect to proceeds collected, including penalties, interest, additions to tax and additional amounts. The amount of the award will be at least 15% but no more than 30% of the collected proceeds in cases in which the Service determines that the information submitted by the claimant substantially contributed to the Service's detection and recovery of tax. If the claimant planned and initiated the actions that led to the underpayment of tax, or to the violation of the internal revenue laws, the Whistleblower Office may reduce the award. If the claimant is convicted of criminal conduct arising from his or her role in planning and initiating the action, the Whistleblower Office will deny the claim.

If an action is based principally on allegations resulting from judicial or administrative proceedings, government reports, hearing, audit, or investigation, or the media, an award of a lesser amount, subject to the discretion of the Whistleblower Office, may be provided; such an award, however, may not exceed 10% of the collected proceeds, including penalties, interest, additions to tax, and additional amounts resulting from the action. This reduction in award percentage does not apply if the Service determines that the claimant was the initial source of the information that resulted in the judicial or administrative proceedings, government reports, hearing, audit, or investigation, or the media's report on the allegations.

3.10 Tax Treatment of Awards

All awards will be subject to current federal tax reporting and withholding requirements. Award recipients will receive a Form 1099 or such other form as may be proscribed by law, regulation or publication.

3.11 Appeal Rights

When the Whistleblower Office has made a final determination regarding a claim, the Whistleblower Office will send correspondence to the claimant regarding its final award determination. Final Whistleblower Office determinations regarding awards under section 7623(b) may, within 30 days of such determination, be appealed to the United States Tax Court. In accordance with section 7623(b)(4), decisions under section 7623(a) may not be appealed to the Tax Court.

3.12 Claims Submitted Prior to Date of Enactment of the Act

Information provided prior to December 20, 2006 (the date of enactment of the Act) is covered by the law and policies in place at the time the information was submitted. Supplemental information provided on or after December 20, 2006, will not be considered a new claim unless its receipt prompts the Service to take an administrative or judicial action that would not otherwise have been taken on the basis of the earlier-supplied information alone.

3.13 Additional Questions

An electronic mailbox for email inquiries has been set up and may be accessed at WO@IRS.gov.

SECTION 4. REQUEST FOR COMMENTS

Interested parties are invited to submit comments on or before February 13, 2008. Comments should be submitted to: Internal Revenue Service, CC:PA:LPD:PR (Notice 2008-4), Room 5203, P.O. Box 7604, Ben Franklin Station, Washington, D.C. 20224. Alternatively, comments may be hand delivered Monday through Friday between the hours of 8:00 a.m. to 4:00 p.m. to: CC:PA:LPD:PR (Notice 2008-4), Courier's Desk, Internal Revenue Service, 1111 Constitution Avenue, N.W., Washington, D.C. Comments may also be submitted electronically via the following email address:

Notice.Comments@irscounsel.treas.gov.

Please include "Notice 2008-4" in the subject line of any electronic submissions.

SECTION 5. EFFECTIVE DATE

This Notice is effective as of January 14, 2008.

SECTION 6. DRAFTING INFORMATION

The principal author of this notice is Holly Styles of the Office of Associate Chief Counsel, General Legal Services. For further information regarding this notice contact Holly Styles at (202) 927-0900 (not a toll-free call).

More Examples of Tax Schemes

Although the ways people commit tax evasion is limitless, this Appendix provides additional examples to help get your juices flowing when looking for unpaid taxes to report.

Other Types of Abusive Trusts

There are many ways people create abusive trusts. Most of the abusive domestic trusts generally fall into three basic schemes, each with a variety of approaches. They are: (1) business trusts; (2) equipment trusts; and (3) family trusts. Although a person can form trusts that do not violate regulations or evade taxes, this section describes when and how these trusts step out of bounds.

Business trusts. The common scheme using a business trust looks like this: A person transfers or places an ongoing business they own into a trust. The purpose of these trusts is to give the appearance that the control of the business has been given to the trust. In reality, the person who transfers it maintains control over the business. They may be a trustee over the trust or control the person they appoint as trustee. Either way, however, the company cannot be sold nor can any major changes be made without that person's approval. In other words, they still run most of the day-to-day activities and definitely control the income stream.

When the person forming the trust maintains control, the IRS does not allow for any tax relief. That person must still claim the income as though no trust existed. These trust schemes go by different names, such as an "unincorporated business organization," a "pure trust," or a "constitutional trust." Regardless of name, the key to determining if the person must claim the income is whether the person still controls the business. If so, they are obligated to pay taxes on the trust income. You can claim a reward if you can show that the trust income was not claimed on tax returns, despite their ability to control the trust.

Equipment trusts. Sometimes a person owns valuable equipment, but does not want to claim the income they receive when renting out such equipment. Therefore, they try to avoid taxes by placing the equipment into an equipment trust. The trust then rents the equipment to a third party or, in the common case of tax fraud, to the person forming the company or a company owned by them. Often, the equipment is rented or leased at inflated rates.

The person forming the trust evades taxes in one of two ways. First, by claiming deductions that would not have been allowable without hiding behind a trust. Second, and more commonly, by using a layering of trusts to disguise true ownership.

The same scheme is often used for services and is called a service trust. For instance, a business provides services to other businesses, such as cleaning services for a large building. The owner of the service company sets up a series of trusts to disguise his ownership of the service company. The trust claims the income from the true client. The trust may also inflate costs or expenses to make it appear that little or no income was made and thus no taxes owed. This is especially true if the person forms a series of trusts relating to the same cleaning contract, with one trust charging the other trust fees for the use of the employees.

Residence trusts. A residence or family trust occurs when a homeowner transfers his residence and furnishings to a trust. The trust claims all of the household expenses as tax deductions, including utilities, maintenance, gardening, pool services, etc. This trust would even claim deductions for depreciation of the house. The trust frequently rents the house back to the person forming the trust.

Consider this example. Claire owns a large home in Arizona. She places the house into a trust, perhaps for her children, but she still maintains control over it. Claire treats the house like a business. The trust pays all of the normal household expenses, including utilities, maid service, pool cleaning, and gardening. The trust creates a rental agreement and charges Claire $5,000 a month in rent. The trust files a tax return claiming the income of $60,000, but deducts $50,000 for all of the expenses incurred. The trust ends up paying tax on just $10,000. These household expenses are not tax deductible to homeowners, but Claire claims that they are business expenses to the trust. Thus, she deducts all of the normal expenses of maintaining and operating the residence. If there were no trust, Claire would have not been able to deduct the $50,000 in household expenses. The point is, hiding behind a trust does not transform costs into allowable deductions.

The IRS will disallow all of the expenses and demand that taxes be paid. The courts have upheld the IRS position when contested by the person forming the trust. Of course, in the example, the amount of underpaid taxes would not exceed $2 million, and thus would be governed under the old Informant Program. You could also report the tax evasion without seeking a reward. The point is to be mindful of the dollar amount of the tax evasion.

The IRS List of Abusive Tax Schemes

There are so many ways that companies cheat on taxes that it would be impractical to list them all. In fact, the IRS has created a list of more than 30 abusive tax schemes.[1] Below are some examples.

Lease In/Lease Out (LILO) Transactions. A person claims to lease property to another, but then turns around and subleases it back. Typically, a friend or family member is involved. They have no real interest in leasing the property. The person leasing the property in the first place has no real interest in leasing it to others, but wants to keep it. They simply want to make it appear that they are leasing property to claim the full-lease value as a deduction, because they cannot claim that amount by merely owning it.

Inflated Partnership Basis Transactions. These are transactions generating losses as a result of artificially inflating the basis of partnership interests. For instance, a person both buys and sells the option to acquire the same stock. They transfer the right to buy

---

[1] They are found on the IRS website at: *http://www.irs.gov/businesses/corporations/article/0,,id=120633,00.html.*

stock to a partnership, and then sell their interest in the company for $0. Even though the initial act of buying and selling options for the stock resulted in no net gain or loss, they claim a loss on the sale of the interest in the partnership. Frequently, accounting firms or other promoters set up the partnership and then coach the person in how to engage in this scheme. The IRS disallows the deduction whenever it becomes aware of it. This is similar to the scheme discussed in Chapter Three where the IRS recovered nearly one-half a billion dollars from an accounting firm and billions from those participants.

Intermediary Transactions. Companies sometimes try to obtain tax deductions for selling certain assets that are not ordinarily tax deductable. Thus, they use an intermediary to sell their assets. They develop agreements with the selling company to make the costs appear to be different than selling assets that would not have been deductible if sold by the company itself.

Transfers of Stock Options to Related Persons. There are many schemes used between related persons who try to avoid claiming income, including transfers of stock options. For instance, transactions between relatives involving compensatory stock options are sometimes used to attempt to avoid federal income and employment taxes.

Lease Strips: There are many variations to lease strips whereby one person claims rental income from one piece of property (or from a service contract) and another person claims the deductions related to the same property (or service contract). Perhaps one person needs to claim more income and the other more deductions so they work in tandem to split the income and expenses from the same property according to their tax situation. Other times, the person claiming the income is not subject to U.S. taxes, so they do not mind having the income attributed to them so the other party can claim the deductions without also claiming the income. This frequently occurs between related parties or a promoter or accountant helps match the people together.

Payroll Tax Fraud

The IRS also cracks down on payroll companies when they cheat. Payroll companies are hired by many small- and medium-sized companies to either prepare payrolls or lease employees to companies.

In most cases, the relationship is perfectly valid and no tax fraud is committed, but a few commit payroll tax fraud. The client companies are not typically part of the fraud, but are simply looking to save time and energy by hiring a company to do the payroll duties. Below is an example of what happens when greed plays a part in the picture.

One professional employment company, which we will call PEC, Inc., had an arrangement with several companies whereby the workers of each of their client companies were treated administratively as employees of the PEC, Inc. On paper, these so-called employees were leased back to the client companies. The client companies liked the arrangement because they would not need to pay for the cost of payroll or collect local, state, and federal taxes from the employees.

In this particular instance, PEC, Inc. had a plan to cheat the IRS. It had 1,000 workers on its payroll and charged its clients fees for leasing the employees to them. It built into the lease the cost the clients would have paid its employees plus a service charge. It was fine to this point; however, PEC, Inc. got greedy. Included into the lease prices were costs meant to cover federal payroll taxes, but PEC, Inc. did not transmit the funds to the IRS. Rather, in a three-year period, it kept $13 million in payroll taxes. It attempted to use some creative accounting devices in an attempt to keep the IRS from figuring out that it was the "employer" of the 1,000 people really working for several smaller companies. The IRS did catch on, and demanded the $13 million, plus penalties and interest.

Failing to pay Excise Tax

Excise tax is a type of tax charged on certain goods produced within the country (as opposed to customs duties, which are charged for goods from outside the country). Typical examples of excise taxes are on gasoline, tobacco, alcohol, certain types of wagering, and highway usage by trucks. Companies that sell these items are required to collect the excise tax on each sale and transmit the funds to the IRS. It is similar to charging state sales tax, but it is an added tax on select items.

In 1995, one trucking company was accused by the IRS of underpaying $160 million in excise taxes over a seven-year period. The company and the IRS reached a settlement. In recent years, the IRS has gone after several companies that concealed excise taxes owed in the ballpark of $10 million.

Factoring of Accounts Receivable

Some businesses discount or "factor" their receivables through deals with related entities that they incorrectly portray as unrelated foreign businesses. Because the two companies are related entities, the transactions are not considered arms length and neither are permitted to use the so-called discounts when preparing tax returns. If discovered, they will face fines and penalties on top of the amount of taxes that were not paid.

Additional Offshore Tax Schemes

International Business Corporations. An International Business Corporation (IBC) scheme seeks to trick the IRS and banks as to the nature of funds to enable them to be moved offshore. For instance, a person establishes a company, referred to as an IBC, with the exact name as their name. In other words, John Doe would create a business named John Doe. He then opens a bank account in a foreign country as John Doe.

As Mr. Doe receives checks from customers, they are made out to John Doe. He sends them to the bank in the foreign country. The foreign bank then uses its correspondent account to process the checks so a customer reviewing his cancelled check will never know that the payments were sent offshore. Once the checks clear, Mr. Doe's account is credited for the check payments. Here the taxpayer has, again, transferred the unreported income offshore to a tax haven jurisdiction. He is able to access the funds in the U.S. by simply using a bank card.

False Billing Scheme. Another variation of the IBC is the false billing scheme. In this situation, John Doe has a person overseas send him invoices for goods which do not exist. This allows Mr. Doe to do two things. First, he can send money offshore without raising red flags. Second, he can claim deductions for the invoices against income. Sadly, there are promoters who help set up these type of schemes for a price.

Asset Management Company. Typically, when a foreign trust package is used, the taxpayer is told by someone promoting foreign trusts to set up an asset management company (AMC). This helps give the appearance that the taxpayer is not really the manager of the assets. Actually they do maintain control. For instance, the promoter may be listed as the trustee on the original documents, but is quickly replaced by the taxpayer.

Next, a business trust is formed, generally in the U.S. Meanwhile, another trust is formed in a tax haven country and the income from the domestic trust is quickly transferred to the foreign trust. This alone would not help the taxpayer, because when the source of income is from the U.S. and the trustee is a citizen, the foreign trust must still file a U.S. tax return.

The final step is where the fraud occurs. A second foreign trust is established. The income from the first foreign trust is transferred to the second foreign trust. Even if a foreign person is the trustee of the second trust, the arrangement is a scam when the original property owner maintains control over that person or the assets, which is the case when tax fraud is involved. However, those promoting the trust tell the taxpayer that he does not need to claim income from the second foreign trust because the sources of income are now foreign and outside the U.S. filing requirements. They may also suggest that it is safe because the IRS cannot obtain information from tax haven countries. Ultimately, these are fraudulent schemes, subject to taxes, and you can help the IRS discover them.

Offshore Deferred Compensation Arrangements. Highly paid executives often want to conceal their huge salaries or bonuses from the IRS. Some have turned to offshore tax fraud. First, on paper they sever their existing employment contract and substitute an arrangement in which a foreign company appears to hire them and lease their services back to the U.S. company. The executive receives a nominal salary from the foreign company, but is granted loans. The executive does not report his true salary, but only the nominal salary provided on paper by the foreign company. Courts have little trouble ruling that these arrangements are shams and that the executive owes taxes and penalties.

Appendix D

Form 211 (Reward Application)

Form 211 (Rev. December 2007)	Department of the Treasury - Internal Revenue Service **Application for Award for Original Information**	OMB No. 1545-0409
		Date Claim Received:
		Claim No. (completed by IRS)

1. Name of individual claimant	2. Claimant's Date of Birth Month Day Year	3. Claimant's SSN or ITIN
4. Name of spouse *(if applicable)*	5. Spouse's Date of Birth Month Day Year	6. Spouse's SSN or ITIN

7. Address of claimant, including zip code, and telephone number

8. Name & Title of IRS employee to whom violation was reported	9. Date violation reported:
10. Name of taxpayer (include aliases) and any related taxpayers who committed the violation:	11. Taxpayer Identification Number(s) (e.g., SSN, ITIN, or EIN):
12. Taxpayer's address, including zip code:	13. Taxpayer's date of birth or approximate age:

14. State the facts pertinent to the alleged violation. (Attach a detailed explanation and all supporting information in your possession and describe the availability and location of any additional supporting information not in your possession.) Explain why you believe the act described constitutes a violation of the tax laws.

15. Describe how you learned about and/or obtained the information that supports this claim and describe your present or former relationship to the alleged noncompliant taxpayer(s). (Attach sheet if needed.)

16. Describe the amount owed by the taxpayer(s). Please provide a summary of the information you have that supports your claim as to the amount owed. (Attach sheet if needed.)

Declaration under Penalty of Perjury
I declare under penalty of perjury that I have examined this application, my accompanying statement, and supporting documentation and aver that such application is true, correct, and complete, to the best of my knowledge.

17. Signature of Claimant

18. Date

MAIL THE COMPLETED FORM TO THE ADDRESS SHOWN ON THE BACK

Form **211** (Rev. 12-2007)   Catalog Number 16571S   publish.no.irs.gov   Department of the Treasury-**Internal Revenue Service**

General Information:
On December 20, 2006, Congress made provision for the establishment of a Whistleblower Office within the IRS. This office has responsibility for the administration of the informant award program under section 7623 of the Internal Revenue Code. Section 7623 authorizes the payment of awards from the proceeds of amounts the Government collects by reason of the information provided by the claimant. Payment of awards under 7623(a) is made at the discretion of the IRS. To be eligible for an award under Section 7623(b), the amount in dispute (including tax, penalties, interest, additions to tax, and additional amounts) must exceed $2,000,000.00; if the taxpayer is an individual, the individual's gross income must exceed $200,000.00 for any taxable year at issue.

Send completed form along with any supporting information to:

Internal Revenue Service
Whistleblower Office
SE: WO
1111 Constitution Ave., NW
Washington, DC 20224

Instructions for Completion of Form 211:
Questions 1 - 7
Information regarding Claimant (informant): Name, Date of Birth, Social Security Number (SSN) or Individual Taxpayer Identification Number (ITIN), address including zip code, and telephone number (telephone number is optional).

Questions 8 - 9
If you reported the violation to an IRS employee, provide the employee's name and title and the date the violation was reported.

Questions 10 - 13
Information about Taxpayer - Provide specific and credible information regarding the taxpayer or entities that you believe have failed to comply with tax laws and that will lead to the collection of unpaid taxes.

Question 14
Attach all supporting documentation (for example, books and records) to substantiate the claim. If documents or supporting evidence are not in your possession, describe these documents and their location.

Question 15
Describe how the information which forms the basis of the claim came to your attention, including the date(s) on which this information was acquired, and a complete description of your relationship to the taxpayer.

Question 16
Describe the facts supporting the amount you claim is owed by the taxpayer.

Question 17
Information provided in connection with a claim submitted under this provision of law must be made under an original signed Declaration under Penalty of Perjury. Joint claims must be signed by each claimant.

Appendix E

Form 2848 (Power of Attorney)

Form **2848** (Rev. June 2008) Department of the Treasury Internal Revenue Service	**Power of Attorney and Declaration of Representative** ▶ Type or print. ▶ See the separate instructions.	OMB No. 1545-0150 **For IRS Use Only** Received by: Name _____ Telephone _____ Function _____ Date / /

Part I Power of Attorney

Caution: *Form 2848 will not be honored for any purpose other than representation before the IRS.*

1 Taxpayer information. Taxpayer(s) must sign and date this form on page 2, line 9.

Taxpayer name(s) and address	Social security number(s)	Employer identification number
	Daytime telephone number ( )	Plan number (if applicable)

hereby appoint(s) the following representative(s) as attorney(s)-in-fact:

2 Representative(s) must sign and date this form on page 2, Part II.

Name and address	CAF No. .... Telephone No. .... Fax No. .... Check if new: Address ☐ Telephone No. ☐ Fax No. ☐
Name and address	CAF No. .... Telephone No. .... Fax No. .... Check if new: Address ☐ Telephone No. ☐ Fax No. ☐
Name and address	CAF No. .... Telephone No. .... Fax No. .... Check if new: Address ☐ Telephone No. ☐ Fax No. ☐

to represent the taxpayer(s) before the Internal Revenue Service for the following tax matters:

3 Tax matters

Type of Tax (Income, Employment, Excise, etc.) or Civil Penalty (see the instructions for line 3)	Tax Form Number (1040, 941, 720, etc.)	Year(s) or Period(s) (see the instructions for line 3)

4 Specific use not recorded on Centralized Authorization File (CAF). If the power of attorney is for a specific use not recorded on CAF, check this box. See the instructions for **Line 4. Specific Uses Not Recorded on CAF** . . . . ▶ ☐

5 Acts authorized. The representatives are authorized to receive and inspect confidential tax information and to perform any and all acts that I (we) can perform with respect to the tax matters described on line 3, for example, the authority to sign any agreements, consents, or other documents. The authority does not include the power to receive refund checks (see line 6 below), the power to substitute another representative or add additional representatives, the power to sign certain returns, or the power to execute a request for disclosure of tax returns or return information to a third party. See the line 5 instructions for more information.

Exceptions. An unenrolled return preparer cannot sign any document for a taxpayer and may only represent taxpayers in limited situations. See **Unenrolled Return Preparer** on page 1 of the instructions. An enrolled actuary may only represent taxpayers to the extent provided in section 10.3(d) of Treasury Department Circular No. 230 (Circular 230). An enrolled retirement plan administrator may only represent taxpayers to the extent provided in section 10.3(e) of Circular 230. See the line 5 instructions for restrictions on tax matters partners. In most cases, the student practitioner's (levels k and l) authority is limited (for example, they may only practice under the supervision of another practitioner).

List any specific additions or deletions to the acts otherwise authorized in this power of attorney: ....

....

....

....

6 Receipt of refund checks. If you want to authorize a representative named on line 2 to receive, **BUT NOT TO ENDORSE OR CASH,** refund checks, initial here _____ and list the name of that representative below.

Name of representative to receive refund check(s) ▶

For Privacy Act and Paperwork Reduction Act Notice, see page 4 of the instructions. Cat. No. 11980J Form **2848** (Rev. 6-2008)

Form 2848 (Rev. 6-2008) Page **2**

7 Notices and communications. Original notices and other written communications will be sent to you and a copy to the first representative listed on line 2.

a If you also want the second representative listed to receive a copy of notices and communications, check this box . . . . . ▶ ☐

b If you do not want any notices or communications sent to your representative(s), check this box . . . . ▶ ☐

8 Retention/revocation of prior power(s) of attorney. The filing of this power of attorney automatically revokes all earlier power(s) of attorney on file with the Internal Revenue Service for the same tax matters and years or periods covered by this document. If you **do not** want to revoke a prior power of attorney, check here . . . . ▶ ☐
YOU MUST ATTACH A COPY OF ANY POWER OF ATTORNEY YOU WANT TO REMAIN IN EFFECT.

9 Signature of taxpayer(s). If a tax matter concerns a joint return, **both** husband and wife must sign if joint representation is requested, otherwise, see the instructions. If signed by a corporate officer, partner, guardian, tax matters partner, executor, receiver, administrator, or trustee on behalf of the taxpayer, I certify that I have the authority to execute this form on behalf of the taxpayer.

▶ **IF NOT SIGNED AND DATED, THIS POWER OF ATTORNEY WILL BE RETURNED.**

Signature	Date	Title (if applicable)

Print Name	PIN Number	Print name of taxpayer from line 1 if other than individual

Signature	Date	Title (if applicable)

Print Name	PIN Number

Part II Declaration of Representative

Caution: Students with a special order to represent taxpayers in qualified Low Income Taxpayer Clinics or the Student Tax Clinic Program (levels k and l), see the instructions for Part II.

Under penalties of perjury, I declare that:

• I am not currently under suspension or disbarment from practice before the Internal Revenue Service;

• I am aware of regulations contained in Circular 230 (31 CFR, Part 10), as amended, concerning the practice of attorneys, certified public accountants, enrolled agents, enrolled actuaries, and others;

• I am authorized to represent the taxpayer(s) identified in Part I for the tax matter(s) specified there; and

• I am one of the following:

a Attorney—a member in good standing of the bar of the highest court of the jurisdiction shown below.

b Certified Public Accountant—duly qualified to practice as a certified public accountant in the jurisdiction shown below.

c Enrolled Agent—enrolled as an agent under the requirements of Circular 230.

d Officer—a bona fide officer of the taxpayer's organization.

e Full-Time Employee—a full-time employee of the taxpayer.

f Family Member—a member of the taxpayer's immediate family (for example, spouse, parent, child, brother, or sister).

g Enrolled Actuary—enrolled as an actuary by the Joint Board for the Enrollment of Actuaries under 29 U.S.C. 1242 (the authority to practice before the Internal Revenue Service is limited by section 10.3(d) of Circular 230).

h Unenrolled Return Preparer—the authority to practice before the Internal Revenue Service is limited by Circular 230, section 10.7(c)(1)(viii). You must have prepared the return in question and the return must be under examination by the IRS. See **Unenrolled Return Preparer** on page 1 of the instructions.

k Student Attorney—student who receives permission to practice before the IRS by virtue of their status as a law student under section 10.7(d) of Circular 230.

l Student CPA—student who receives permission to practice before the IRS by virtue of their status as a CPA student under section 10.7(d) of Circular 230.

r Enrolled Retirement Plan Agent—enrolled as a retirement plan agent under the requirements of Circular 230 (the authority to practice before the Internal Revenue Service is limited by section 10.3(e)).

▶ **IF THIS DECLARATION OF REPRESENTATIVE IS NOT SIGNED AND DATED, THE POWER OF ATTORNEY WILL BE RETURNED.** See the Part II instructions.

Designation—Insert above letter (a–r)	Jurisdiction (state) or identification	Signature	Date

Form **2848** (Rev. 6-2008)

Appendix F

Sample IRS Letter

Whistleblower Office
[Seal]

                    Department of the Treasury
                    Internal Revenue Service
                    Washington, D.C. 20224

                         (date)

Name of Attorney for Whistleblower
Address
City and State

Dear Mr. xxxxx:

We received the Form 211 you submitted on behalf of Mr. John Doe and it has been assigned claim number xx-xxxxx.

The information you provided will be evaluated to determine if an investigation is warranted and an award is appropriate. Although we may need to contact you to discuss the information submitted, we cannot tell you specific details about what actions we are taking, if any, using the information you gave us. Internal Revenue Code Section 6103 protects the tax information of all taxpayers and prevents us from making these disclosures. At the conclusion of the review and investigation, we will only be able to tell you whether or not the information you provided met our criteria for paying an award.

Should you have any questions, Whistleblower Office analyst Ms. Xyz has been assigned to your claim and can be reached at (xxx) xxx-xxxx.

                    Sincerely,

                    Jane Doe
                    Senior Advisor, Whistleblower Office

cc: Ms. Xyz

Appendix G
DOJ Guidelines for Reward Amounts

Below is the text of the Department of Justice Guidelines for determining the exact percentage of award to a whistleblower.

December 10, 1996
Relator's Share Guidelines

Section 3730(d)(1) of the False Claims Act ("FCA"), 31 U.S.C. §§ 3729-33, provides that a *qui tam* relator, when the Government has intervened in the lawsuit, shall receive at least 15 percent but not more than 25 percent of the proceeds of the FCA action depending upon the extent to which the relator substantially contributed to the prosecution of the action. When the Government does not intervene, section 3730(d)(2) provides that the relator shall receive an amount that the court decides is reasonable and shall be not less than 25 percent and not more than 30 percent.

The legislative history suggests that the 15 percent should be viewed as the minimum award—a finder's fee—and the starting point for a determination of the proper award. When trying to reach agreement with a relator as to his share of the proceeds, or proposing an amount or percentage to a court, we suggest that you begin your analysis at 15 percent. Then consider if there are any bases to increase the percentage based on the criteria set forth below. Having done this, consider if that percentage should be reduced based on the second set of criteria. Of course, absent one of the statutory bases for an award below 15 percent discussed at the end of these guidelines, the percentage cannot be below 15 percent (or 25 percent if we did not intervene).

Items for consideration for a possible increase in the percentage.
1. The relator reported the fraud promptly.
2. When he learned of the fraud, the relator tried to stop the fraud or reported it to a supervisor or the Government.
3. The *qui tam* filing, or the ensuing investigation, caused the offender to halt the fraudulent practices.
4. The complaint warned the Government of a significant safety issue.
5. The complaint exposed a nationwide practice.
6. The relator provided extensive, first-hand details of the fraud to the Government.
7. The Government had no knowledge of the fraud.
8. The relator provided substantial assistance during the investigation and/or pre-trial phases of the case.
9. At his deposition and/or trial, the relator was an excellent, credible witness.
10. The relator's counsel provided substantial assistance to the Government.
11. The relator and his counsel supported and cooperated with the Government during the entire proceeding.
12. The case went to trial.
13. The FCA recovery was relatively small.
14. The filing of the complaint had a substantial adverse impact on the relator.

Items for consideration for a possible decrease in the percentage
1. The relator participated in the fraud.
2. The relator substantially delayed in reporting the fraud or filing the complaint.
3. The relator, or relator's counsel, violated FCA procedures:
    a. complaint served on defendant or not filed under seal.

  b. the relator publicized the case while it was under seal.

  c. statement of material facts and evidence not provided.

4. The relator had little knowledge of the fraud or only suspicions.

5. The relator's knowledge was based primarily on public information.

6. The relator learned of the fraud in the course of his Government employment.

7. The Government already knew of the fraud.

8. The relator, or relator's counsel, did not provide any help after filing the complaint, hampered the Government's efforts in developing the case, or unreasonably opposed the Government's position in litigation.

9. The case required a substantial effort by the Government to develop the facts to win the lawsuit.

10. The case settled shortly after the complaint was filed or with little need for discovery.

11. The FCA recovery was relatively large.

These items are not meant to be an exhaustive list of the criteria one should consider when trying to determine an appropriate award for a relator, but they do constitute many of the factors that routinely should be considered. Finally, please note that section 3730(d)(1) limits the relator to no more than 10 percent of the proceeds when the complaint is based primarily on public information and that section 3730(d)(3) allows the court to reduce the percentage below 15 percent if the relator planned and initiated the fraud and requires the court to dismiss the relator if he is convicted for the actions giving rise to the submission of the false claims.

More about Other Government Reward Programs

The IRS Reward Program is not the only game in town. The federal government and dozens of states have programs paying significant rewards to citizens for reporting other types of fraud against the government. The author has written a separate book about these reward programs, with step-by-step instructions. It is named, *Whistleblowing: A Guide to Government Reward Programs (How to Collect Millions of Dollars for Reporting Fraud)* (2007). Below is a short description of those reward programs.

Rewards for Reporting Fraud against the Federal Government

The federal government pays rewards of up to 25% of the funds it recovers. This includes reporting fraud against the military, Medicare, and Homeland Security. The program is not limited to these more well-known programs, but applies to any government contract and any federal agency, including the Postal Service. Many states have similar programs. Below are some facts about the DOJ Reward Program:

- $3 billion in rewards have already been paid
- $150 million is the largest reward to date
- $1.5 million is the average reward
- 10% of all government spending is lost to fraud
- 1 out of 5 whistleblowers receive a reward

The DOJ whistleblower reward program is working remarkably well, having recovered over $20 billion and paying out nearly $3 billion in rewards to citizens. However, most Americans are still unaware of this robust program.

Examples of Federal Fraud Cases

There are many ways companies and individuals cheat under federal government contracts, grants, or programs. Below are some cases in which the Department of Justice has paid out significant rewards to citizens who reported fraud. Of course, the ways people cheat are numerous. Merely because a type of fraud is not listed below does not mean DOJ is not interested.

- Medicare and Medicaid fraud
- Fraud against the military, homeland security and other federal agencies
- Pharmaceutical fraud
- Postal Service fraud
- Underpaying royalties owed, i.e. gas, oil, minerals
- Grant fraud (research/educational)
- Guaranteed Loan Program fraud
- Trade Agreement Act or Buy America violations
- Customs fraud
- Housing fraud
- TINA (Truth in Negotiations Act) fraud
- GSA fraud

State Reward Programs

Many states have passed whistleblower reward statutes modeled after the Department of Justice reward statute. The growing list includes: California, Delaware, District of Columbia, Florida, Georgia, Hawaii, Illinois, Indiana, Louisiana, Massachusetts, Michigan, Montana, Nevada, New Hampshire, New Jersey, New Mexico, New York, Oklahoma, Rhode Island, Tennessee, Texas, Virginia and Wisconsin. More states are expected to join this constantly growing list, and information regarding state reward programs will be updated on the author's website *(www.HowToReportFraud.com)*.

The state reward programs work largely the same as the federal DOJ Reward Program, with one primary difference. These programs apply when there is fraud against the state, as opposed to the federal government. The same technical requirements for the federal program are applicable. In fact, courts often look to the federal reward program for guidance in deciding how to interpret the state laws. That is why it is so important to understand the federal program. These state programs also require you to hire counsel and submit formal legal documents.

Examples of State Fraud

The state reward statute is a perfect supplement to the DOJ Reward program because there are many instances where the loss to the government occurs solely through state funds.

The following state cases paid significant rewards in context other than Medicaid:

- A large bank chain improperly kept proceeds relating to $187 million in municipal bonds.
- A local electric company cheated Los Angeles schools by overcharging them $160 million for electricity.
- A company overcharged a state government by $43 million relating to the installation and monitoring of heating and cooling systems in state buildings.
- A company sold $30 million in defective computers to the state.
- A company cheated by $30 million during the construction of the Los Angeles subway system.
- A hospital falsely reported the amount of its charity work and engaged in kickbacks totaling $14 million.
- A company sold to nursing homes $4 million in "repackaged" drugs that had been returned, but not used. (This violated certain rules and regulations.)

Appendix I
Additional Resources

IRS Report Critical of the Old Informant Reward Program

The Inspector General for the Department of Treasury evaluated the IRS Informant Program in 2006 and issued a critical report named, "Treasury Inspector General for Tax Administration, The Informant's Rewards Program Needs More Centralized Management Oversight (June 2006)." The report can be located at the following website:

> *http://www.ustreas.gov/tigta/auditreports/2006reports/*
> *200630092fr.pdf*

IRS Information Regarding its Reward Program

The IRS issued publications to assist whistleblowers in understanding the program requirements, which are located on its website:

> *http://www.irs.gov/newsroom/article/0,,id=176632,00.html*
> *http://www.irs.gov/pub/irs-pdf/p733.pdf*

IRS Defining Abusive Trusts

The IRS describes "abusive foreign trusts" on its website:

> *http://www.irs.gov/businesses/small/article/0,,id=106559,00.html*
> *http://www.irs.gov/businesses/small/article/0,,id=106541,00.html*

Reporting Tax Evasion Anonymously

The IRS website provides information on how to report tax evasion without seeking a reward, even anonymously:

http://www.irs.gov/individuals/article/0,,id=106778,00.html

Reporting Tax Preparers Who Commit Abuse

The IRS website provides information on how to report misconduct about someone preparing tax returns or giving advice on abusive tax schemes:

http://www.irs.gov/irs/article/0,,id=175512,00.html

Reporting Abuse by an IRS Employee, or Waste and Abuse

The IRS website provides information on how to confidentially report to the Treasury Inspector General for Tax Administration (TIGTA) an instance of misconduct, waste, fraud or abuse by an IRS employee or a tax professional, or you can call 1-800-366-4484 (1-800-877-8339 for TTY/TDD users):

http://www.treas.gov/tigta/contact_report.shtml

IRS Information Regarding the Statute of Limitation

A good IRS publication relating to SOL can be found at:

http://www.irs.gov/pub/irs-tege/epch1102.pdf

Glossary

Civil Fraud Section of the Department of Justice (aka Civil Frauds).
A division of the Department of Justice in Washington, D.C., responsible for handling fraud and False Claims Act cases and overseeing the DOJ Reward Program. Generally, the Civil Fraud Section has responsibility over all fraud or False Claims Act cases over $1 million. Cases below that amount are within the primary authority of the United States Attorney's office located throughout the United States. However, the United States Attorney often works jointly with the Civil Fraud Section on the larger cases. Conversely, the Civil Fraud Section frequently assists the United States Attorney with cases below this amount. In short, the two offices often combine efforts and make a formidable team. (*See also* DOJ Reward Program, United States Attorney.)

Department of Justice (DOJ). The United States Department of Justice (DOJ) is a Cabinet department in the United States government. As part of the executive branch of the government, DOJ is the chief enforcer of federal laws and defender of the interests of the United States. Its roles include ensuring fair and impartial administration of justice for all Americans. The DOJ is administered by the United States Attorney General in Washington, D.C., together with the U.S. Attorneys located throughout the country. There are many divisions and subsections of DOJ, one of which is the Civil Fraud Section, which oversees and is primarily responsible for administering the federal whistleblower program under the False Claims Act. (*See also* Civil Frauds, U.S. Attorney's Offices.)

Department of Justice (DOJ) attorneys. The term DOJ Attorneys is used to describe Civil Fraud Section attorneys and Assistant U.S. Attorneys assigned to fraud cases. There are several branches of the government with responsibility for investigating and pursuing fraud allegations. The DOJ attorneys with the Civil Fraud Section pursues civil fraud claims against any federal agency or program, such as Medicare and the military. However, they do not have authority over collection of federal taxes. Rather, the IRS agents and IRS attorneys are responsible for tax fraud and tax evasion. However, neither the DOJ attorneys in the Civil Division nor the IRS attorneys have authority over criminal sanctions, which is conducted solely by the Criminal Division of DOJ. Thus, the Criminal Division of DOJ is responsible for criminal prosecution of tax fraud. But, the Criminal Division attorneys do not have any responsibility for either the DOJ Reward Program or the IRS Reward Program. The DOJ attorneys in the Civil Division administer the DOJ Reward program, including collecting back the amount of loss due to fraud and paying whistleblower rewards. The Whistleblower Office of the IRS is responsible for administering the IRS Reward program, and uses IRS agents and IRS attorneys. (*See also* Civil Frauds, DOJ Reward Program, IRS Whistleblower Reward Program, Whistleblower Office, United States Attorney.)

Department of Justice (DOJ) Reward Program. This is the short-hand way of describing the federal reward program under the False Claims Act statute, which pays rewards to whistleblowers filing *qui tam* complaints. The IRS Whistleblower Reward Program is modeled after the DOJ Reward Program. (*See also* Complaint, False Claims Act, IRS Whistleblower Reward Program, Whistleblower.)

Excise Tax. Excise tax is a type of tax charged on certain goods produced within the country (as opposed to customs duties which charge for goods from outside the country). Typical examples of excise taxes are on gasoline, tobacco, alcohol, wagering, and highway usage by trucks.

False Claims Act (FCA). This is the name of the statute which, among other things, authorizes private citizens to apply for rewards for reporting fraud against the government under the DOJ Reward Program. The statute can be found at 31 United States Code §§3729-3733. (*See also* Complaint, DOJ Reward Program, Whistleblower.)

Freedom of Information Act (FOIA). A federal statute which allows any person the right to obtain documents held by federal agencies unless the records are protected from disclosure by an exemption in the law.

Fraud. Fraud is a generic term used to describe certain classes of misconduct. Broadly speaking, it is an intentional misrepresentation or a deception made for personal gain. The specific legal definition varies by jurisdiction, with some states requiring proof of each of as many as nine elements: (1) a representation; (2) falsity of the representation; (3) materiality of the representation; (4) speaker's knowledge of the falsity of the representation; (5) the speaker's intent which should be relied upon; (6) the hearer's ignorance of the falsity of the representation; (7) the hearer's reliance on the representation; (8) the hearer's right to rely on the representation; and (9) the hearer's consequent and proximate injury caused by reliance on the representation. In most civil lawsuits, the person alleging fraud must also provide clear and convincing evidence (a standard higher than in most civil cases) of the misconduct. The IRS Whistleblower Reward Program does not require proving fraud. However, there is no statute of limitation if the IRS proves fraud, i.e. specific intent to evade taxes. (*See also* Statute of Limitation.)

Government Accountability Office (GOA). This is a non-partisan audit, evaluation, and investigative arm of Congress. The GAO was originally named the General Accounting Office. It is designed to "investigate, at the seat of government or elsewhere, all matters relating to the receipt, disbursement, and application of public funds, and shall make to the President ... and to Congress ... reports [and] recommendations looking to greater economy or efficiency in public expenditures."

IRC or Internal Revenue Code. Generally, the statute relating to the IRS is known s the IRC, and is located in volume 26 of the United States Code (U.S.C.). The IRC section relates to the same section number in the USC under volume 26. For instance, IRC Section 6501 means 26 U.S.C. Section 6501.

Internal Revenue Service (IRS). The governmental agency responsible for collecting federal taxes and conducing audits relating to income tax filings. (*See also* IRS Whistleblower Reward Program.)

IRS Whistleblower Reward Program. Rather than relying almost exclusively upon audits, the IRS recently overhauled its sagging whistleblower reward program, which now pays 15% to 30% of the amount the IRS recovers in unpaid taxes based upon reports by citizens. It is modeled largely after the DOJ Reward Program. It is also referred to as the IRS Reward Program. It is administered through the IRS Whistleblower Office. (*See also* DOJ Reward Program.)

IRS Form 211. This is the IRS Form a whistleblower must fill out and sign to be eligible for a reward. It is known as an Application for Reward for Original Information. A copy is attached at Appendix C.

IRS Form 2848. This is the IRS Form a whistleblower must fill out and sign if they are using the help of an attorney. Unless this form is submitted to the IRS, the IRS will not speak to your attorney. It is known as "Power of Attorney and Declaration of Representation." A copy is attached at Appendix D.

IRS Form 1099. When a whistleblower receives a reward under one of the three government reward programs, the agency issues an IRS Form 1099 to the citizen. It is similar to a W2 issued to employees. The Form 1099 is also sent to the IRS office that maintains files regarding income of taxpayers. The whistleblower must claim the reward as income when filing annual income tax forms. (*See also* Whistleblower, IRS Whistleblower Reward Program.)

IRS Attorneys. The IRS uses its own attorneys to investigate and pursue civil claims of tax evasion and tax fraud, whereas, under the DOJ Reward Program, allegations of fraud against a federal agency are investigated and pursued by attorneys with the Civil Division of the Department of Justice. If the IRS opens up a tax evasion or tax fraud case, it is assigned to an IRS attorney, with assistance by IRS agents. However, criminal prosecution of tax fraud is conducted by the Criminal Division of the DOJ. (*See also* DOJ Attorneys, IRS agents.)

IRS Agents. As used in this book, the term IRS agent means investigators with the IRS that are specially trained to detect and investigate fraud or tax evasion. The term does not include an agent of the IRS which conducts routine tax audits. IRS agents assist the assigned IRS attorney on a particular tax evasion or tax fraud matter and help collect taxes. The IRS Whistleblower Office is responsible for paying whistleblower rewards. (*See also* DOJ Attorneys, IRS Attorneys, Whistleblower Office.)

IRS Whistleblower Office. The Whistleblower Office of the IRS was created in December 2006 by Congress mandate, and the first named Director was Stephen Whitlock. The IRS Whistleblower Office is a section within the IRS, but maintains a certain level of autonomy. The Whistleblower Office is responsible for determining if a tax evasion investigation is warranted and a whistleblower reward appropriate. The office also determines the amount of rewards paid. If a whistleblower receives an award, but thinks it is too low, the amount can be appealed to the tax court. The Whistleblower Office must provide annual reports to Congress. The office is located in the main Internal Revenue Service building at 1111 Constitution Ave., N.W., Washington, D.C. 20224. (*See also* Whistleblower Reward Program.)

Medicaid. Medicaid is the combined federal and state health insurance program for individuals and families with low incomes and resources. It is jointly funded by the federal and state governments. Each state manages the program within its borders. Examples of those eligible for Medicaid are low-income parents, children, seniors, and people with disabilities. Centers for Medicare and Medicaid Services (CMS) monitors the program from the federal perspective. When a person or company cheats Medicaid, both the federal and state governments can bring actions to recover back the funds. The government annually spends $500 billion for this program.

Medicare. Medicare is the federal government program which acts as a health insurance program. It covers people who are either age 65 and over, or who meet other special criteria. It was originally enacted on July 30, 1965. Currently, the federal government spends nearly $500 billion each year on this program. Medicare is administered by the Centers for Medicare and Medicaid Services (CMS) [formerly HCFA], which hires carriers and fiscal intermediaries to run the program.

Public disclosure bar. Under government reward programs, including the IRS Reward Program, the amount of a reward paid to a whistleblower can be eliminated or reduced if it is determined that the same information has already been publicly disclosed in the media or certain government reports. However, there are significant exceptions to the public disclosure bar if the whistleblower can show that he meets the definition of an "original source" of the information. The courts have not uniformly ruled upon what this exception means or when it applies and it is important for your attorney to be a strong advocate. Under the DOJ program, if the whistleblower has first-hand knowledge of the information provided—perhaps due to the fact that he is an employee of the company that is cheating and has learned the information directly—he typically can satisfy the exception. Refer to Chapter Seven for a discussion related to the IRS Reward Program.

Qui tam (qui tam **lawsuit).** This term is derived from the Latin phrase, meaning "he who pursues a matter on behalf of the king, as well as for himself." (The most common pronunciation of the term *qui tam* is "kwee tom," but it is often sounded out as "key tam" or "kwee tam.") A person desiring to apply for a DOJ Reward must file a civil lawsuit, which is often referred to as a *qui tam* lawsuit, as part of the application process. Generally, a person must hire a lawyer to file a *qui tam* lawsuit. Some courts have ruled that a *qui tam* lawsuit filed without being signed by an attorney must be dismissed and DOJ has never paid a significant reward to any person who did not use the services of an attorney to file a *qui tam* suit. (*See also* Complaint, DOJ Reward Program, Whistleblower.) The IRS Reward Program is different. It does not require a person to file a formal suit to be eligible for a reward. However, there are other technical requirements, including filing out Form 211, for eligibility for an IRS whistleblower reward.

Relator. Not to be confused with a "realtor," who sells property, this term is the modern name for a whistleblower. It refers to the person filing a *qui tam* lawsuit under the DOJ Reward Program. The term "relator" is derived from the fact that the person is one who *relates* information to the government that fraud is afoot. (*See also* Whistle-blower, *qui tam*, DOJ Reward Program.) The IRS Reward Program does not use this term. Rather, it considers the person a whistleblower.

Settlement. This refers to when the parties reach a monetary settlement of a lawsuit or *qui tam* case. A whistleblower is allowed to share in the proceeds of settlements under all three government reward programs. (*See also* Complaint, DOJ Reward Program, *qui tam*.)

Statute of limitation (SOL). The time within which a lawsuit must be filed or the right to file the lawsuit is lost. Under the IRS Reward Program, the statute of limitation is three years for most instances of underpaid taxes, and six years for other matters. See Chapter Eight. However, if the IRS can establish that the person intentionally cheated, i.e. possessed specific intent to defraud, there is no statute of limitation. In order for a whistleblower to be eligible for a reward, they must file the application before the SOL expires. A good IRS publication relating to SOL can be found at: *http://www.irs.gov/pub/ irs-tege/epch1102.pdf.*

State reward program. Many states have adopted reward programs which mirror the DOJ Reward Program, with the primary difference that it applies to fraud under state contracts and programs instead of fraud against the federal government. (*See also* Complaint, DOJ Reward Program, *qui tam*, Whistleblower.)

Tax evasion. This is a shorthand way of saying that a person or company underpaid taxes. It does not denote that they acted intentionally. Rather, when a person intends to cheat on taxes, that is referred to as tax fraud. The distinction is very important because there is no statute of limitation on tax fraud; whereas the statute of limitation for tax evasion is as short as three years. In addition, the level of proof differs greatly. To establish tax evasion, it is only necessary to show that taxes are owed. For instance, if a person received tax advice from an accountant and it turned out to be wrong, they would still be required to pay the taxes. A whistleblower is entitled to receive a reward in those instances, provided the statute of limitation has not expired. To establish tax fraud, however, the IRS must show that the person or entity intended to cheat. The distinction is discussed in Chapter Eight. (*See also* Tax Fraud, Statute of limitation.)

Tax Fraud. The term refers to when a person or company intentionally underpaid taxes. It requires a showing that the person or entity knew that they owed taxes, but did not report or pay them. The distinction between this and tax evasion is very important because there is no statute of limitation on tax fraud; whereas the statute of limitation for tax evasion is as short as three years. In addition, the level of proof differs greatly. To establish tax evasion, it is only necessary to show that taxes are owed. To establish tax fraud, the IRS must show that the person or entity intended to cheat. The distinction is discussed in Chapter Eight. (*See also* Tax Evasion, Statute of limitation.)

U.S. Attorney's Offices. The United States Attorneys serve under the direction of the United States Attorney General of the Department of Justice. (*See* Department of Justice). There are 93 United States Attorneys stationed throughout the United States and its territories.

United States Attorneys are appointed by, and serve at the discretion of the President of the United States, with advice and consent of the United States Senate. One United States Attorney is assigned to each of the judicial districts. The U.S Attorney is part of the Department of Justice. Each U.S. Attorney's Office has a team of Assistant United States Attorneys who handle criminal and civil actions on behalf of the United States for matters occurring within their jurisdiction either alone or jointly with Department of Justice attorneys from the main headquarters in Washington, D.C. They are also known as federal prosecutors. With respect to fraud or False Claims Act matters, the Civil Fraud Section of the Department of Justice in Washington, D.C. is primarily responsible for the DOJ Reward Program, but works closely with the U.S. Attorneys Offices on most cases. The False Claims Act requires a whistleblower to serve a copy of the *qui tam* complaint upon both the Civil Fraud Section and the local U.S. Attorney where the allegations occur. (*See also* Civil Fraud Section, Department of Justice, and DOJ attorneys.)

Whistleblower. A whistleblower is someone willing to step forward and report that a person or company has not paid the full amount of taxes owed to the federal government. It is often an employee who reveals wrongdoing within an organization to the public or to those in positions of authority. The IRS Reward Program sometimes refers to the person as an informant. When a whistleblower follows the correct procedures and meets the requirements, they are entitled to a reward.

Whistleblower Reward (IRS Whistleblower Reward). Under the IRS Reward Program, when a whistleblower follows the correct procedures and meets all of the requirements, they are generally entitled to a reward of between 15% and 30% of what the IRS collects based upon their information. Refer to Chapter Seven for a discussion related to ranges of rewards.

Index

About the Author

For more than 15 years (1990–2006), Joel Hesch served as a Trial Attorney with the Civil Fraud Division of the Department of Justice (DOJ) in Washington, D.C. This is the office responsible for the modern day DOJ Whistleblower Reward Program, after which the IRS modeled its Reward Program.

Mr. Hesch spent over 25,000 hours directly analyzing and pursuing alleged fraud against 20 different federal agencies under the DOJ Whistleblower Reward Program. The cases he worked on resulted in over a billion dollars ($1,000,000,000.00) in judgments and recoveries, and paid more than $250 million in rewards to average citizens for reporting fraud.

For his efforts, Mr. Hesch received numerous awards from the Justice Department, including a Special Commendation Award for outstanding service, a Meritorious Award for superior service, and two Special Achievement Awards for sustained and superior performance of duty in combating fraud. In addition, he received an award from NASA for fighting fraud under the NASA Space Shuttle Program.

The Director of the Civil Frauds Section made these statements in Mr. Hesch's work appraisals:

> "As has been true for many years, Mr. Hesch continues to show dedication to the office's mission of combating fraud and to working selflessly on whatever cases can best utilize his talents. We recognize and appreciate his fine efforts.... Mr. Hesch is a delightful colleague and has the ability to work well on a team as well as independently.... Mr. Hesch has significantly exceeded expectations."

At the end of fiscal year 2006, Mr. Hesch left a rewarding career with DOJ to become a law school professor. Since then, he has written scholarly law review articles suggesting standards for the government and courts to follow when deciding whether a whistleblower can still receive a reward although the allegations have previously appeared in the news media. One of his articles was cited five times in a brief to the United States Supreme Court. Mr. Hesch also submitted an *amicus* brief with the United States Supreme Court arguing in favor of a whistleblower claiming a reward for reporting fraud.

Mr. Hesch now represents whistleblowers who are interested in claiming a reward for reporting tax evasion under the IRS Reward Program and those reporting fraud under the DOJ Reward Program and similar state reward programs.

How to Ask Mr. Hesch to Consider Your Case

If you think you have a case that is eligible for a reward under the new IRS Reward Program and want to ask Mr. Hesch to consider representing you, please refer to his website , *www.HowToReportFraud. com* for information.

Updates

Mr. Hesch maintains an informative website which contains statistics and updates to the IRS Reward Program. See *www.HowTo ReportFraud.com*.

CPSIA information can be obtained at www.ICGtesting.com
Printed in the USA
BVOW04s1615120214

344712BV00003B/337/P